Collins

Key Stage 3

World Religions: Judaism, Christianity and Islam

Robert Orme and Andy Lewis

Series Editor: Robert Orme

T0382077

William Collins' dream of knowledge for all began with the publication of his first book in 1819. A self-educated mill worker, he not only enriched millions of lives, but also founded a flourishing publishing house. Today, staying true to this spirit, Collins books are packed with inspiration, innovation and practical expertise. They place you at the centre of a world of possibility and give you exactly what you need to explore it.

Collins. Freedom to teach

Published by Collins

HarperCollins Publishers
1 London Bridge Street
London
SE1 9GF

HarperCollins Publishers
Macken House
39/40 Mayor Street Upper
Dublin 1, D01 C9W8
Ireland

Text © Robert Orme and Andy Lewis 2017
Design © HarperCollins*Publishers* 2017

10 9

ISBN 978-0-00-822768-5

A catalogue record for this book is available from the British Library

Publisher: Joanna Ramsay
Editor: Hannah Dove
Authors: Robert Orme and Andy Lewis
Series Editor: Robert Orme
Development Editor: Sonya Newland
Project Manager: Emily Hooton
Copy-editor: Jill Morris
Image researcher: Shelley Noronha
Proof-readers: Ros and Chris Davies and Nikky Twyman
Cover designer: We Are Laura
Cover images: Dewitt/Shutterstock; Zoran Karapancev/ Shutterstock; bogdan ionescu/Shutterstock
Production controller: Rachel Weaver
Typesetter: QBS

This book contains FSC™ certified paper and other controlled sources to ensure responsible forest management.

For more information visit: www.harpercollins.co.uk/green

Contents

Introduction

It is not easy to define what makes something a religion. In some religions one god is worshipped, in others many gods are worshipped, and in some no god is worshipped at all. Some religions have a single founder. In others, there is not one person who starts it or one clear moment when it began. To make things more complicated, there are often strong differences of opinion between and even within particular religions. Two people following the same religion can believe opposing things and follow their religion in strikingly different ways. Within any religion, some people build their whole lives around their beliefs while others are less committed to their religion but still think of themselves as part of it. Followers of all religions believe that they have found truth, but their ideas about what is true differ greatly.

Approximately 84 per cent of people in the world today follow a religion and experts predict that this will rise to 87 per cent by 2050. The most followed religion in the UK is Christianity, but there are also followers of many other religions including Islam, Judaism, Buddhism, Hinduism and Sikhism. In recent times there has also been a big increase in the number of people in the UK who do not follow any religion. Some are atheists which means that they do not believe there is a god or gods. Others are agnostics meaning they are not sure if a god or gods exists. Others might believe there is a god or gods, but choose not to belong to a religion.

By studying the beliefs and ways of life of millions of people around the world, you will gain a greater understanding of the past, the modern world and humanity itself. You will explore questions that have troubled humankind through the ages and examine the diverse ways in which these questions have been answered. In a world where religion has and continues to play such a large role, the importance of understanding it is as great as ever.

Robert Orme (Series Editor)

Concise topic introductions set the scene and focus your learning.

Engaging photos illustrate the key ideas.

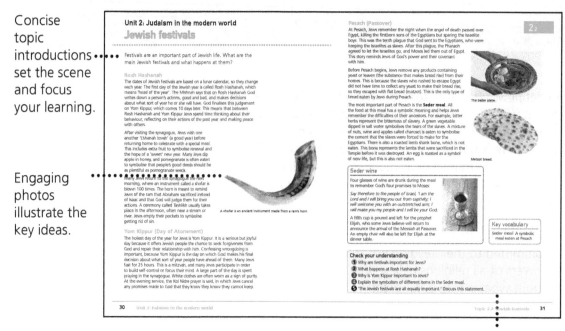

End-of-topic questions are designed to check and consolidate your understanding.

Key vocabulary lists for each unit help you define and remember important terms.

Key fact boxes help you to revise and remember the main points from each unit.

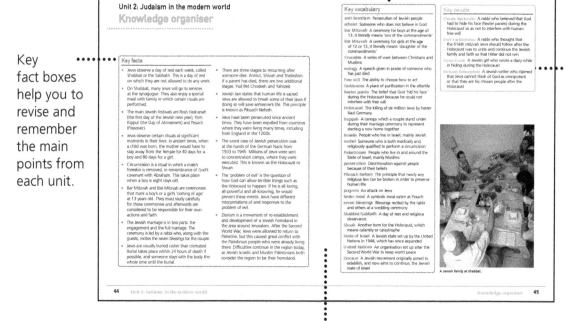

Key people boxes summarise the key figures from the unit.

Knowledge organisers can be used to revise and quiz yourself on key dates, definitions and descriptions.

Judaism

History and belief

In this book, you will find out about one of the most influential and ancient religions on earth – Judaism. In the first half of the book, you will discover how Judaism began and explore some of the main ideas which shape the religion. You will find out why the city of Jerusalem is so important to Jews as well as examine the different ways that Jews understand the idea of the Messiah. Finally, you will explore how Jews worship, pray and follow the many laws that they believe God has given to them.

Unit 1: History and belief

What is Judaism?

Judaism has played a significant role in human history, but when did it begin, and how does it continue to give significance to the lives of many millions of people?

Some religions begin with a single founder at a specific moment. Others develop gradually over a period of time. Jewish beliefs about how Judaism began are based on its most holy text, the **Torah**. According to the Torah, approximately 4000 years ago God made a **covenant** with a man called Abraham who lived in a city called Ur Kasdim, in what is now Iraq. God told Abraham that he had chosen him and his descendants to be a great nation of people who would have a special relationship with him.

Originally, the descendants of Abraham were known as Hebrews, or Israelites. People began to call them Jews about 2700 years ago. This was because many of them were living in a southern part of Israel called Judah. Today, Jews still believe that they are physical and spiritual descendants of Abraham, and that they have a special relationship or covenant with God.

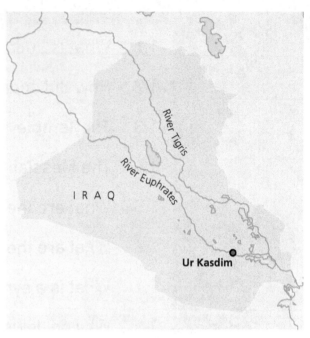

This map shows the location of Ur Kasdim, where Abraham is believed to have lived about 4000 years ago.

Although Judaism is a very old religion, it is quite small. There are approximately 14 million Jews in the world, which is 0.2 per cent of the world's population. The country with the largest Jewish population is Israel, which is home to over 6 million Jews (75 per cent of the country's total population). There are also just under 6 million Jews in the USA and approximately 270,000 in the UK.

> **Fact**
>
> Jews meet to worship God in buildings called **synagogues**. The leader of a synagogue is called a **rabbi**, which means teacher.

What do Jews believe about God?

Jews are **monotheists**, which means they believe in one God. They consider God to be eternal, meaning he has no beginning or end, and that he is the creator of everything. Jews also believe that God is almighty – that he is very powerful – and that he is a good, loving God. Many Jews believe that the name of God is so holy that it should not be spoken or written. They often write 'G-d', or use names like 'Adonai' ('My Lord') or 'Hashem' ('The Name') instead.

What is the Tanakh?

The main Jewish scriptures are called the **Tanakh**, or sometimes the Hebrew Bible, because Hebrew is the language in which they were originally written. The Tanakh is divided into three sections. The most

Country	Jewish population
Israel	6,399,000
USA	5,300,000
France	465,000
Canada	385,000
UK	269,568
Russia	186,000
Argentina	181,000
Germany	99,695
Australia	112,500
Brazil	95,000

This table shows the 10 countries in the world with the highest population of Jews.

important is the Torah, which comes first. The Torah teaches Jews about how their religion began and the laws that God wants them to follow as part of their special covenant relationship. Jews tend not to be too focused on what happens after we die. Their focus is on living a good and holy life in the present. They believe that if they obey God's laws he will look after them.

Different types of Jews

Unlike many other religions, people are born into Judaism. Even if someone does not follow the religion, he or she may still be Jewish. Jews who do not believe in God are called **secular** Jews. Unlike some Christians and Muslims, Jews do not try to convert people to their religion. It is possible to convert to Judaism if there is a good reason, such as marriage, but the process can be long and difficult.

Orthodox Jews are one group of Jews. They believe it is essential to keep traditional beliefs and the Jewish way of life alive. Orthodox Jews think that the laws in the Torah show clearly how God wants Jews to live and should be closely followed. About half of Jews in Britain are Orthodox, and there are approximately 300 Orthodox synagogues. **Conservative Jews** are not as strict and traditional as Orthodox Jews. Although they preserve Jewish rituals and traditions, they are more flexible in interpreting Jewish laws in the modern world.

Hasidic Jews such as those in this image are part of Orthodox Judaism.

There are other groups of Jews known as **Reform Jews** and **Liberal Jews**. These two groups are different, but they share a view that Jewish belief and worship can change or modernise over time. For example, some Reform synagogues allow women to be rabbis, while Orthodox synagogues do not. Reform and Liberal Jews might also think that some of the laws in the Torah are not appropriate for today because they reflect the times in which they were written rather than how God wants people to live now.

Key vocabulary

Conservative Jews Jews who preserve Jewish rituals and traditions but are more flexible in interpreting Jewish laws than Orthodox Jews

covenant An agreement between God and people

Liberal Jews A group of Jews who believe that Judaism can change or modernise over time

monotheist Someone who believes in just one God

Orthodox Jews Jews who believe in maintaining the traditional beliefs and practices of Judaism and the laws given by God

rabbi The leader of a synagogue

Reform Jews A group of Jews who believe that Judaism can change or modernise over time

secular Non-religious

synagogue The Jewish place of worship

Tanakh The main Jewish scripture, which includes the Torah

Torah The most important holy text for Jews

Check your understanding
❶ How did Judaism begin?
❷ How many Jews are there in the world today?
❸ Explain what Jews believe about God.
❹ What is the Tanakh?
❺ Explain why there are different groups of Jews today.

How did Judaism begin?

The story of Judaism begins with three men known as the patriarchs. Who were they, and what do Jews believe about them?

Jews believe that nearly 4000 years ago, in the Middle East, God chose a man named Abraham to begin a new religion based on the radical idea of worshipping one God. Abraham was the first patriarch (founding father of Judaism). The second patriarch was Abraham's son Isaac, and the third was Isaac's son and Abraham's grandson, Jacob. These three men are believed to be the physical and spiritual ancestors of all Jews.

Who was Abraham?

Abraham lived around 4000 years ago. At this time, most people were **polytheists** – they believed in many gods. They sacrificed animals and occasionally humans to try and please their gods. It was also common to worship **idols**. Originally, Abraham was a polytheist, but during his life he came to believe that there was only one God, who had created everything. This was a very different belief from the polytheistic ideas of people in the Middle East, as well as other ancient civilisations.

According to the Torah, God tested Abraham in ten different ways to see how strong his faith was. In the first test, God told Abraham to leave his home in Ur. This was a difficult thing for Abraham to do because he was living a good and happy life, but he agreed. God made a covenant with Abraham, saying he would bless him and make his family a great nation. God told Abraham that all of the males in Abraham's family must be **circumcised** in order to show this special relationship.

Who was Isaac?

Abraham thought that his wife Sarah was too old to have a baby, so he had a son with his wife's servant, Hagar. Their son was called Ishmael. However, Sarah also fell pregnant and gave birth to a son, named Isaac. God tested Abraham again, telling him to take Isaac to a place called Mount Moriah and to kill him on a **sacrificial altar**. Although Abraham had waited a long time to have a child, he travelled to the mountain with Isaac, and showed that he was willing to obey God. Just as Abraham was about to plunge his knife into his son, an angel of the Lord appeared and stopped him. Abraham had passed God's test.

> **Fact**
>
> According to Jewish tradition, Abraham's father sold idols for a living, but Abraham destroyed these when he started to believe in one God.

Abraham and his son Isaac climbing Mount Moriah.

Who was Jacob?

Isaac had twin sons, Jacob and Esau. Jacob had 12 of sons of his own. During Jacob's lifetime, there was a drought throughout the land, and so he travelled to Egypt with his large family. They settled in Egypt and lived happily there for many years. God changed Jacob's name to Israel and the families of his sons became known as the **Twelve Tribes of Israel**.

Who was Moses?

Abraham's descendant Moses is another important figure in Judaism. By the time of Moses, Jacob's descendants, the Israelites, were being forced to work for the Egyptians as slaves. God told Moses to free the Israelites and lead them to the land that God had promised them.

At first, the **Pharaoh** refused to let the Israelites go, so God sent 10 plagues to Egypt. The final plague was an angel of death that killed all the firstborn sons in Egypt, including Pharaoh's oldest son. After this, he agreed to free the slaves, and Moses led them through the desert to the Red Sea. When they reached the water, God parted it so that they could pass through. The Israelites lived in the desert for 40 years before they finally settled in the **Promised Land**. During this time, God gave Moses the Ten Commandments – ten laws that the Israelites had to follow – on Mount Sinai. They are still very important for Jews today.

> **Fact**
>
> Abraham is an important person in Christianity and Islam as well as Judaism. These religions are sometimes called the Abrahamic or monotheistic faiths.

> **Key vocabulary**
>
> **circumcision** The removal of a baby boy's foreskin at the age of eight days in Judaism
>
> **idols** Statues that are worshipped
>
> **Pharaoh** An Egyptian king
>
> **polytheist** Someone who believes in more than one god
>
> **Promised Land** An area of land in the Middle East given to Jews by God
>
> **sacrificial altar** A place where animals were killed as offerings to God
>
> **Twelve Tribes of Israel** The families of the sons of Jacob

Moses parting the Red Sea.

> ### Check your understanding
> 1. Approximately when did Judaism begin?
> 2. Who were the patriarchs?
> 3. Describe the beliefs of people who lived in the Middle East 4000 years ago.
> 4. Describe the life of Abraham.
> 5. Why is Moses an important figure in Jewish history?

The Temple

What is the Temple and why is it so important to Jews?

Particular places often have a special significance to followers of different religions. The Western Wall in Jerusalem is the most important site in the world for Jews. It is the remaining wall of a place called the Temple, in which their ancestors worshipped.

The First Temple

According to the Tanakh, King David (who ruled about 3000 years ago) had wanted to build a Temple to house the **Ark of the Covenant**, but it was not constructed until the reign of his son, King Solomon. The Temple was the only place where certain rituals such as animal sacrifices were performed, and most Jews would try to visit at least once a year, even if this required days of travelling.

Destruction of Temple of Jerusalem by Emperor Titus.

The First Temple was attacked on several occasions and was finally destroyed by the Babylonians between 586 and 587 BCE. The Jews themselves were captured and forced to live outside their homeland under Babylonian rule. This is known as the **Babylonian exile**. During this time, the Ark of the Covenant was lost.

The Second Temple

The Babylonian exile lasted for 59 years. After this, the Jews returned to Jerusalem and rebuilt the Temple. Historians are not sure exactly what this Temple was like, but sources including the Christian New Testament, the **Mishnah** and the writings of a Jewish historian called Josephus give us some idea.

Jerusalem had a population of around 150,000 at this time, but during important Jewish festivals more than a million people might crowd into the city. Originally, the Second Temple was probably quite modest, but to cope with these crowds the Roman governor, Herod, extended it into a huge, wondrous building, sometimes called 'Herod's Temple'. Parts were made from

> ### Fact
>
> Non-Jews sometimes refer to the Western Wall as the 'Wailing Wall'. This name comes from a time when Jews were banned from the city apart from one day a year, when they were allowed to cry at the ruins. Many Jews consider this name to be offensive.

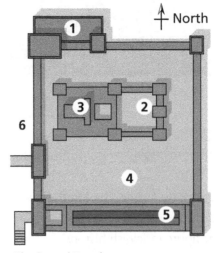

North

The Second Temple

1 Antonia Fortress
2 Inner Temple Precincts
3 Holy of holies
4 Court of the Gentiles
5 Royal Stoa
6 Western Wall

gold, and large bronze doors led to areas for making sacrifices, worship, socialising and studying.

At the centre of the Second Temple was the Holy of Holies, which was where the Ark of the Covenant had once been kept. With the Ark lost, this was left empty in the Second Temple. Only the High Priest was allowed in the Holy of Holies, and even then only on one special day of the year.

The Temple today

In 70 CE, the Temple was destroyed again, this time by the Romans. Today, the only part of the building that remains is a wall known as the Western Wall (*Kotel* in Hebrew). The earliest mentions of this as a place of **pilgrimage** for Jews are from the sixteenth century CE. Jews visiting the Western Wall often write prayers and put them into cracks between the stones.

A Jewish boy praying at the Western Wall.

The site of the Temple, including the Holy of Holies, is now occupied by Islamic buildings: the Dome of the Rock (a Muslim shrine) and the Al-Aqsa Mosque. Mosques are often built on holy sites, and Muslims believe that the Prophet Muhammad ascended into heaven from here. Since 1967, Jewish–Israeli authorities have had control of the Wall and the space in front of it, but over the past 100 years there has been much tension between Muslims and Jews in Jerusalem.

Rebuilding the Temple

In the fourth century CE, the Roman Emperor Julian began to have the Temple rebuilt. However, an earthquake brought work to a standstill, and the building was abandoned. Some Jews believe that the Temple will be rebuilt in the future and pray three times a day for this to happen, but some Jews reject the idea of rebuilding it. They believe that their synagogues are adequate places for worship and prayer.

Activity

Using the information on these pages, draw a timeline to show the history of the Temple in Jerusalem. If you can, find out more about it, and add some dates. You could illustrate it with suitable pictures from the internet.

Key vocabulary

Ark of the Covenant The box that housed the two tablets of stone on which the original Ten Commandments were written

Babylonian exile The period from 597 to 538 BCE when Jews were forced to live outside Jerusalem under Babylonian rule

Mishnah The early teachings of rabbis, which were passed on orally

pilgrimage A journey taken to a place of religious importance

Check your understanding

1. What was the First Temple built to house?
2. Why might some people refer to the Second Temple as 'Herod's Temple'?
3. When and by whom were the two Temples destroyed?
4. What is the Western Wall?
5. Why is the rebuilding of the Temple a controversial issue?

The Messiah

What do Jews believe about the Messiah?

Originally, the term **Messiah** was used to describe a ceremony in which a man was anointed with holy olive oil and crowned as king. This act was done by a **prophet** or the **High Priest**. Later, Jews started using the word Messiah to mean a future king who would rule over them. According to the Tanakh, the Messiah would return Jews to Israel, bring peace, build the Third Temple and have a son who would be his heir. Some Jews are still waiting for this Messiah to come.

Jews believed that the Messiah would be a descendant of King David.

The Messianic Age

Some Jews believe that the arrival of the Messiah will be the start of a period of time known as the Messianic Age. According to the Tanakh, war will end, and all people will live in peace and harmony. It will be a time of freedom in which the covenants God made with the Jews will be restored forever. A book of the Tanakh called Micah has a verse (4.3) that describes this time:

> ❝ He will judge between many peoples and will settle disputes for strong nations far and wide. They will beat their swords into ploughshares and their spears into pruning hooks. Nation will not take up sword against nation, nor will they train for war any more. ❞

The 13 Principles of Faith

Orthodox Jews believe that they must uphold the 13 Principles of Faith, which were written by a rabbi called Maimonides in medieval times. One of these principles – number 12 – refers to the Messiah: 'I believe with perfect faith in the coming of the Messiah and even though he tarries, with all of that I await his arrival with every day.' This belief has helped sustain Jews through some of their darkest times. Many Jews executed by the Nazis during the Holocaust (see pages 40–41) recited these words as they went to their deaths.

Has the Messiah come already?

Although the Christian Bible describes Jesus as a descendant of David, Jews do not believe that he was the Messiah. They do not think that he fulfilled the mission described in the Tanakh, nor do they believe that the Messiah will be divine, as Christians believe Jesus was.

Bar Kokhba means 'Son of the Star', which comes from a prophecy about the Messiah in the Hebrew Bible.

Some Jews believed that a man called Shimeon ben Kosiba, known as Bar Kokhba, who lived about 100 years later than Jesus, more closely matched the description of the Messiah. He was a strong and charismatic leader who helped free Jerusalem from the Romans and restart worship and sacrifice at the site of the Temple. However, he was eventually killed by the Romans, and Jews decided that he was not the Messiah.

Modern Jewish views

Orthodox Jews believe that the Messianic Age will come in the future, as stated in the 13 Principles of Faith. Some Orthodox Jews, especially a group called **Hasidic Jews**, believe that there is one person in each generation who has the potential to be the Messiah and who will try to bring about the Messianic Age.

However, other Jews are reluctant to make any claims about the Messiah. They believe it is impossible to say what the Messianic Age will be like and allow individuals to make up their own minds. Many Reform Jews do not accept the idea of a Messiah, yet think the idea of a Messianic Age is a positive thing and that Jews should work towards a world where there is greater peace. Discussion of the Messiah does not play a big role in much of modern Judaism.

> **Fact**
>
> Hasidic Jews follow a strict religious lifestyle and have a distinctive appearance. They wear black clothes and do not cut the hair at the sides of their head (called payot) or their beards.

Hasidic Jewish men often wear a black hat and on special occasions some married men may wear a fur hat called a shtreimel.

> **Key vocabulary**
>
> **Hasidic Jews** A group within Orthodox Judaism who follow a strict religious lifestyle and have a distinctive appearance
>
> **High Priest** Historically, the highest rank of Jewish leader
>
> **Messiah** Anointed one
>
> **prophet** A messenger of God

Check your understanding

1. What does the word 'Messiah' mean?
2. Describe Jewish beliefs about the Messianic Age.
3. Why do Jews not believe that Jesus was the Messiah?
4. Who was Shimeon ben Kosiba and how did he match some of the descriptions of the Messiah?
5. Explain different modern Jewish perspectives on the Messiah.

Unit 1: History and belief
What are the Tanakh and Talmud?

What are the most sacred texts for Jews, and why are they so important?

The Tanakh

Jewish scriptures are known as the Tanakh, or sometimes the Hebrew Bible. The Tanakh is divided into three sections:

- the Torah (the books of law)
- the Nevi'im (the books of the prophets)
- the Ketuvim (the books of writings).

The Torah

For Jews, the most important section of the Tanakh is the Torah. This contains five books: Genesis, Exodus, Leviticus, Numbers and Deuteronomy. The Torah explains the 'laws' that Jews must follow. In all, there are 613 laws, known as **mitzvot**. Some laws tell Jews how they should worship and what festivals they should observe. Others offer more general advice on how to live in ways that will please God.

Orthodox Jews try to keep as many of these mitzvot as possible. Conservative Jews will keep many, but may reinterpret some laws for modern life. However, Reform and Liberal Jews think that many of the laws are too difficult to keep, or are not relevant in the modern world. They believe that the Torah was not just revealed once, but is continuously being revealed to Jews. This means that how Jews lived in the past is not necessarily how they should live today.

The yad helps readers keep their place as they recite from the Torah.

In synagogues, a handwritten copy of the Torah is kept on a scroll. It is written in Hebrew, the language in which it was originally recorded. It is a great honour to be asked to read from the Torah in a synagogue, but to do so a Jew must first learn Hebrew. The person reading from the Torah uses a pointing stick with a hand on it called a **yad** so that no fingers damage the holy scroll. When it is not being used, the Torah is stored in the **Ark**.

The Nevi'im

The Nevi'im teaches Jews about the history of their religion as well as the words of their prophets. Jews believe that the prophets had special knowledge from God. This meant that they could tell people how God wanted them to behave, and sometimes they gave people strong warnings about their ways of life.

Parts of the Nevi'im are read during synagogue services, but they are usually read from a book rather than written on a scroll. Many parts of the Nevi'im are only read at home or for personal study.

The Ketuvim

The Ketuvim contains important stories from Jewish history. The section that Jews use most is the book of Psalms. This contains songs that praise God and make requests of him. They were written over a period of around 500 years by a number of authors, including King David and King Solomon. The psalms were first used by the Jews who worshipped in the Temple in Jerusalem.

The Talmud.

The Talmud

The **Talmud** is a collection of teachings from rabbis compiled from around 200 to 500 CE, around 2500 years after the time of Abraham. It is made up of two parts, the Mishnah (the early teachings of rabbis, which were passed on orally) and the **Gemara**, a commentary on the Mishnah. These give lots of additional detail about the laws in the Torah, helping explain them so that Jews know how to live. The Talmud is sometimes referred to as the 'Oral Tradition' because the teachings were originally passed from rabbi to rabbi by word of mouth.

Other writings

Other important writings for Jews include the **Midrash**, which includes rabbis' interpretations of and further information about the Torah, Jewish law and moral issues. There are also books of response, 'responsa', which are answers to questions focused on Jewish law. The world today is very different from the world in which Judaism began, so these are still being written to help Jews respond to the challenges of modern life that their ancestors did not face.

The Tishbi, a dictionary containing words used in the Talmud and Midrash.

Key vocabulary

Ark a cupboard in a synagogue where Torah scrolls are stored

Gemara Part of the Talmud, a commentary on the Mishnah

Midrash Jewish writings that include rabbis' interpretations of and further information about the Torah, Jewish law and moral issues

mitzvot Jewish laws (there are 613 in total); the singular is mitzvah

Talmud A collection of teachings from rabbis giving more information about the Torah

yad A pointer used to read the Torah in the synagogue

Check your understanding

❶ What is the Tanakh?

❷ Why is the Torah considered the most important collection of books for Jews?

❸ What is the Talmud?

❹ Explain how a Jew today might use each of the different books mentioned in this topic.

❺ Why might the responsa help Jews today?

What are the mitzvot?

What laws do Jews live by and what do they believe about these laws?

There are 613 Jewish laws, known as mitzvot ('commandments' in Hebrew). These were given to Moses by God in order to teach Jews the best way to live. Those who follow the commandments will be rewarded and those who disobey them will be punished. We often think of rules as things that can cause difficulties, but Jewish scholars suggest that the mitzvot are a gift given to help Jews.

Study of the Torah including the mitzvot is an important part of life for Jews.

Interpretations of the mitzvot

Jews believe that they should follow the mitzvot because these laws have come from God and honouring them will deepen their relationship with him. Orthodox Jews believe that the Torah is the literal word of God, so the mitzvot should be followed at all times. This can present many challenges, particularly as some of the mitzvot mention the Temple in Jerusalem, which was destroyed nearly 2000 years ago.

Reform Jews have a different view. They believe that the mitzvot were from an ancient time and that not all of the laws are relevant today. They think it is acceptable to follow the mitzvot selectively and that God allows rabbis to reinterpret them for the modern world.

The mitzvot cover a wide range of topics. For example, they tell Jews that they should look after those in need and show acts of kindness. These acts may include visiting the sick, feeding the hungry or comforting mourners.

Jewish food laws

There are many food laws (**kashrut**) in Judaism. The Torah and Talmud both provide detailed guidance on how to keep these laws. Orthodox Jews try to observe all the rules of kashrut; Conservative Jews will keep many, but perhaps reinterpret some for the modern day. Reform and Liberal Jews will observe some of the laws.

Food that is acceptable to eat is described as **kosher**, which means 'fit' or 'correct'. Any food that is not kosher is described as **trefah** ('torn' in Hebrew). The Torah includes instructions about what food is acceptable and what is not. For example, eating pig meat is forbidden, and so most Jews will not eat pork. In order for meat to be kosher, the animal has to be killed by a kosher slaughterer. It is essential that this is done quickly, by making a deep cut in the animal's jugular vein (in the neck). Before the meat is eaten, all remaining blood must be drained from the meat.

Some scholars have suggested that in ancient times food laws had health benefits for Jews. For example, pigs carried diseases, so it made sense to not eat them. Also, not eating animals that were unconscious before being killed reduces the risk of eating an unhealthy animal.

> ❝ [26]See, I am setting before you today a blessing and a curse – [27]the blessing if you obey the commands of the Lord your God that I am giving you today; [28]the curse if you disobey the commands of the Lord your God and turn from the way that I command you today by following other gods, which you have not known. ❞
>
> Deuteronomy 11.26–28

Fact

If a Jewish person accidentally breaks kashrut, he or she might try to make amends by giving to charity, fasting or praying to God.

Mixing meat and dairy

The Torah states that some combinations of food are not acceptable. In Exodus 23.19 it says 'Do not cook a young goat in its mother's milk,' so Jews do not eat meat and dairy products at the same time. After eating meat, they usually wait either three or six hours before eating dairy. This means that a cheeseburger or a chicken curry containing cream would be trefah. However, a curry made with coconut milk would be kosher. After eating meat, a Jew would wait before having a milkshake or a cup of tea containing milk.

Orthodox Jews will usually have separate cutlery and crockery for meat and dairy products and if possible two sinks in their kitchen. Jewish food laws can cause problems when eating out – cooking methods as well as the food have to be kosher. This means that some Jews choose to eat out only in kosher restaurants. Usually, kosher restaurants are either dairy or meat restaurants. In a meat restaurant, the deserts will not include dairy products; for example, they may replace butter with margarine, which is made with oil.

> ❝ Any animal that has divided hoofs and is cleft-footed and chews the cud – such you may eat. ❞
> Leviticus 11.3

A kosher restaurant in Paris.

Some kosher symbols that are found on food.

Key vocabulary

kashrut Jewish food laws

kosher Food that is acceptable for Jews to eat; the word literally means 'fit'

trefah Food that Jews are forbidden to eat

Activity

Draw up a table with two columns. On one side list types of food and drink that are considered kosher and on the other types that are trefah. Try to include a variety of foods such different meats, fish and cheese.

Check your understanding

1 What is the origin of the mitzvot?
2 Why do Jews follow the mitzvot?
3 How do groups of Jews differ in their views about mitzvot?
4 Explain the kashrut that Jews follow.
5 'Jewish food laws are outdated and irrelevant.' Discuss this statement.

What is a synagogue?

Where do Jews go to worship and what happens during their religious services?

Jews worship in a synagogue, a word that means 'bringing together'. This is a fitting name, because Jews meet here as a community in order to learn about their ancestors and think about how God wants them to live. The connection between Jews and their family and friends throughout history is a very important part of the religion.

The Ark

The most important part of every synagogue is the Ark. This is a cupboard where the Torah is kept. The Ark is usually built into a wall that faces Jerusalem. This reminds Jews of the Holy of Holies in the Temple, where the Ark of the Covenant was stored. Above the Ark is the **ner tamid**, which means 'eternal light'. This is a light that is kept burning above or in front of the Ark at all times. It reflects God's eternal nature and the idea that the Jewish family will be everlasting. It also reminds Jews of the **menorah** that burned in the Temple.

The bimah

As well as an Ark, synagogues always have a **bimah** – a raised platform where the rabbi stands when leading the service. During a service, the Torah scrolls are taken from the Ark to the bimah and read from there. The **congregation** sits below the bimah, symbolising how the Torah is higher than humans. The design of synagogues reflects the Temple in Jerusalem, and the bimah represents the sacrificial altar.

In an Orthodox synagogue, women usually sit separately from men, as they did in the Temple. This is generally at the back of the synagogue or on a balcony. They may sit separately in Conservative synagogues too. In Reform and Liberal synagogues everyone sits together.

As well as a rabbi, who leads the service, there is often a cantor, who leads the music and singing. In Orthodox synagogues the cantor must be a man, but in Conservative, Liberal and Reform synagogues it may be a woman.

Conservative, Liberal and Reform synagogues also have female rabbis, but the vast majority of Orthodox communities do not. Members of the community may also help with parts of the service, for example, reading from the Torah. The main prayer book used in synagogues is called the **siddur**. It is written in Hebrew, but an English translation is also available in many synagogues.

North ←——|

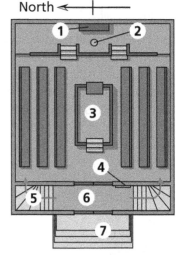

1 Ark containing the Torah
2 Ner tamid
3 Bimah
4 Memorial
5 Stairs up to women's gallery
6 Entrance hall and stairs
7 Porch

A plan of the inside of an Orthodox synagogue. Liberal or Reform Jews sometimes adapt buildings that were previously used for something else, and so their synagogues can have slightly different layouts.

The star of David is included on the flag of Israel.

The outside (and inside) of a synagogue may also be decorated with symbols. Two of the most important symbols in Judaism are the menorah and the star of David. The origins of the star of David are unknown, but it has been used for hundreds of years. The menorah symbolises divine light in the world. Some synagogues also have stained-glass windows like Christian churches and they sometimes contain artwork inside.

Famous synagogues

The oldest ruins of a synagogue were found on the Greek island of Delos. It is thought to have been built in around 150 BCE. The oldest synagogue in the world still in use is the Old New Synagogue of Prague in the Czech Republic, built in the 1270s. The Bevis Marks Synagogue is the oldest synagogue in the UK. It was built in London in 1701 and is the only synagogue in Europe to have held services continually for over 300 years.

One of the most famous synagogues in the world is the Hurva synagogue in Jerusalem. It has been destroyed on two occasions (1721 and 1948) and was most recently rebuilt in 2010.

Activity

In pairs, discuss why you think the synagogue is important for Jews.

Fact

Nobody is certain when Jews first started meeting in synagogues, but it was probably during the Babylonian exile. At this time Jews were living outside Jerusalem and could no longer worship in the Temple because it had been destroyed.

Key vocabulary

bimah The platform from where Torah scrolls are read

congregation People who attend a religious service

menorah A seven-branched candlestick and a symbol of divine light in the world

ner tamid The light in front of, or above, the Ark

siddur A Jewish prayer book

Check your understanding

1. What does the word 'synagogue' mean and why is this a fitting name?
2. Explain why some synagogues are different from others.
3. How might congregations be seated in different synagogues?
4. Who are the key people in a synagogue?
5. Describe the main features of a synagogue and explain what they are or what they symbolise.

Unit 1: History and belief
Why do Jews pray?

Prayer is an important part of Judaism, but how and why do Jews pray?

Many practising Jews pray three times a day: in the morning, afternoon and evening. Some Jews attend a synagogue every day for these prayers, but for most Jews this is not practical, so they will pray at home instead. Jews may also pray at many other times throughout the day.

There are many reasons why Jews pray. They may want to praise and thank God, to ask him for something or just to keep him at the forefront of their minds. Self-reflection is an important part of prayer for Jews and when Jews pray privately they usually do so silently. The main goal of all prayer is to build the relationship between the individual and God.

Dressed for prayer

While praying, men will usually cover their heads with a **kippah** to show respect to God. In some Jewish traditions, women also wear a kippah while they are praying. Men may wear a shawl called a **tallit**, which has 613 tassels to remind them of all the commandments in the Torah. By wrapping themselves in a tallit, Jews show that they wish to wrap themselves in God's will. Wearing it also helps them to focus on prayer. They may also strap two small boxes, called **tefillin**, to themselves, one to the forehead and the other on an arm. Each box contains verses from the Torah. They are worn to help focus the person's mind and heart on prayer.

An African Jew wearing a kippah.

Public prayer

Since the destruction of the Temple, daily prayers in local synagogues are seen as the most important act of Jewish worship. These prayers remind Jews that they are all part of an ancient community. In most synagogue services there are set prayers. These are written down so they can be recited by everyone together and are taken from the siddur.

In order for Jewish prayers to be recited and for the Torah to be read, there needs to be a minyan present. A minyan is a group of 10 people aged 13 or over. Praying together publicly helps create a sense of unity with both those present and the global Jewish community. This is because Jews know that others around the world are taking part in similar services and saying the same prayers as them. In an Orthodox synagogue, prayers will often be recited in Hebrew, but in other traditions of Judaism there is often a mixture of Hebrew and the local language.

A Jew in Israel wearing tefillin and a tallit.

The Shema

The most important prayer for Jews is called the **Shema**, which is a summary of what Jews believe. It is usually said twice a day – during morning and evening daily prayers. The Shema can often be found on doorposts in Jewish homes, in a small container called a **mezuzah**. When Judaism began, most people were polytheists. The Shema declares that there is only one God and that Jews should love him with their whole being and follow his laws. The first part is considered the most important, and is the part that is used most often:

Jews praying at the Western Wall.

Hear, O Israel, the Lord is our God, the Lord is One.
Blessed be the name of the glory of His kingdom forever and ever.
You shall love the Lord your God with all your heart, with all your soul, and with all your might. And these words which I command you today shall be upon your heart. You shall teach them thoroughly to your children, and you shall speak of them when you sit in your house and when you walk on the road, when you lie down and when you rise. You shall bind them as a sign upon your hand, and they shall be for a reminder between your eyes. And you shall write them upon the doorposts of your house and upon your gates.

Deuteronomy 6.4–9

Key vocabulary

kippah A head covering worn during prayer

mezuzah A small box attached to doorposts in Jewish homes, containing the Shema

Shema The most important prayer in Judaism

tallit A symbolic shawl worn during prayer

tefillin Two boxes worn during prayer, which contain verses from the Torah

A mezuzah.

Check your understanding

1 How often do most practising Jews pray?

2 Why do Jews pray?

3 Explain why praying in the synagogue is important for Jews.

4 Explain what the Shema could teach someone about Jewish beliefs.

5 'There is no point praying.' Discuss this statement, with reference to Judaism.

Unit 1: History and belief
Knowledge organiser

Key vocabulary

Ark a cupboard in a synagogue where Torah scrolls are stored

Ark of the Covenant The box that housed the two tablets of stone on which the original Ten Commandments were written

Babylonian exile The period from 597 to 538 BCE when Jews were forced to live outside Jerusalem under Babylonian rule

bimah The platform from where Torah scrolls are read

circumcision The removal of a baby boy's foreskin at the age of eight days in Judaism

congregation People who attend a religious service

Conservative Jews Jews who preserve Jewish rituals and traditions but are more flexible in interpreting Jewish laws than Orthodox Jews

covenant An agreement between God and people

Gemara Part of the Talmud, a commentary on the Mishnah

Hasidic Jews A group within Orthodox Judaism who follow a strict religious lifestyle and have a distinctive appearance

High Priest Historically, the highest rank of Jewish leader

idols Statues that are worshipped

kashrut Jewish food laws

kippah A head covering worn during prayer

kosher Food that is acceptable for Jews to eat; the word literally means 'fit'

menorah A seven-branched candlestick and a symbol of divine light in the world

Messiah Anointed one

mezuzah A small box attached to doorposts in Jewish homes, containing the Shema

Midrash Jewish writings that include rabbis' interpretations of and further information about the Torah, Jewish law and moral issues

Mishnah The early teachings of rabbis, which were passed on orally

mitzvot Jewish laws (there are 613 in total); the singular is mitzvah

monotheist Someone who believes in just one God

ner tamid The light in front of, or above, the Ark

Orthodox Jews Jews who believe in maintaining the traditional beliefs and practices of Judaism and the laws given by God

Pharaoh An Egyptian king

pilgrimage A journey taken for religious reasons

Pilgrimage A journey taken to a place of religious importance

polytheist Someone who believes in more than one god

Promised Land An area of land in the Middle East given to Jews by God

prophet A messenger of God

rabbi The leader of a synagogue

Reform Jews and **Liberal Jews** Jews who believe that Judaism can change or modernise over time

sacrificial altar A place where animals were killed as offerings to God

secular Non-religious

Shema The most important prayer in Judaism

siddur A Jewish prayer book

synagogue The Jewish place of worship

tallit A symbolic shawl worn during prayer

Talmud A collection of teachings from rabbis giving more information about the Torah

Tanakh The main Jewish scripture, which includes the Torah

tefillin Two boxes worn during prayer, which contain verses from the Torah

Torah The most important holy text for Jews

trefah Food that Jews are forbidden to eat

Twelve Tribes of Israel The families of the sons of Jacob

yad A pointer used to read the Torah in the synagogue

Key facts

- The origins of Judaism go back about 4000 years, when God made a covenant with Abraham to make him leader of God's chosen people. They were known originally as Israelites, but were later called Jews.

- God tested Abraham's faith by asking him to sacrifice his son Isaac. Abraham was willing to do so and God spared Isaac.

- Jews view Abraham as the first patriarch. Isaac was the second patriarch and his son Jacob was the third. Moses is also an important figure for Jews.

- The Temple was the most important place for Jews. Built by King Solomon, it was destroyed by the Babylonians, but later rebuilt. The Romans destroyed the Second Temple. One wall remains, known as the Western Wall.

- There are different types of Jews, including Orthodox, Reform and Liberal Jews, who believe slightly different things and practise Judaism in different ways.

- Jews believe that the coming of a Messiah, or saviour, will mark the start of a new age when people will live in peace and harmony. Unlike Christians, Jews do not believe that Jesus was the Messiah.

- The two most important scriptures for Jews are the Torah (part of the Tanakh) and the Talmud (a collection of writings by rabbis).

- Jewish law is known as the mitzvot – a collection of 613 rules and instructions on how Jews should live their lives.

- There are strict laws about what Jews can eat. Permitted food is called kosher ('fit'). Food that is banned is known as trefah ('torn').

- Jews worship in buildings called synagogues. The most important part of the synagogue is the Ark – a special cupboard where the Torah is kept.

- When Jews pray, they may wear particular items of clothing that have special meaning: a kippah (head covering), tallit (shawl) and tefillin (two small boxes strapped to the forehead and arm).

Key people

Abraham A man who God made a covenant with that he would have many descendants who would be a great nation

Herod A Roman governor who built an extension to the Second Temple

Isaac The son of Abraham and the second patriarch

Jacob The son of Isaac and the third patriarch

Moses A man who received the laws including the Ten Commandments from God

Solomon The king of Israel who built the first Temple in Jerusalem

Jews praying together publicly.

Judaism in the modern world

The world today is very different from the way it was when Judaism began. Jews around the world now face challenges that people in the past did not have to consider. In the second half of this book you will see how Jews respond to these challenges and keep their faith strong. You will also discover how Judaism has survived extreme persecution over the course of its long history and explore how its followers have tried to make sense of the suffering that they have experienced. Finally, you will examine the role that Judaism plays in one of the most complex conflicts in the modern world. As you study more about Judaism, you will gain a greater understanding of the past, the modern world and the lives of millions of people around the world who call themselves Jews.

What is Shabbat?

Keeping the ancient tradition of **Shabbat** alive is an important part of following God's law and keeping the Jewish community strong. How do Jews do this?

A day of rest

Once a week, Jews stop their normal activities and have a day of rest. This is called Shabbat, or the **Sabbath**. Shabbat literally means 'ceasing'. Shabbat begins at sunset on Friday evening and ends one hour after sunset on Saturday evening. This means that the exact timings change throughout the year. Orthodox Jews use a special calendar that tells them when Shabbat should start and end. Some Reform Jews may choose to observe Shabbat from 6.00 p.m. on Friday to 6.00 p.m. on Saturday.

What are the origins of Shabbat?

The idea of Shabbat comes from the book of Genesis in the Torah, which says that God created the world in six days and rested on the seventh day. In the second book of the Torah, Exodus, Moses receives the Ten Commandments from God on Mount Sinai. The fourth commandment is to observe Shabbat. As such, keeping Shabbat is an important part of following God's law, and continues a tradition that dates back thousands of years. In the modern world different Jews observe Shabbat in different ways.

> ❝ Six days you shall labour and do all your work; but on the seventh day, which is a Sabbath in honour of the Lord your God, you shall not do any work. ❞
>
> Exodus 20.9–10

What counts as work?

The Torah describes 39 types of action as work, so these are all forbidden on Shabbat. If something is not mentioned, Jews will try to decide if it counts as work or not, but there is not always agreement. Orthodox Jews follow the rules about not working very strictly. They may switch off electronic devices such as mobile phones and will not use their car or even public transport. Because of this, Orthodox Jews often live within walking distance of the synagogue, where they spend Shabbat. Reform Jews often argue that it is more important to attend the synagogue than not drive a car. It is common for Reform Jews to refer to their rabbi for advice on what counts as work in the modern world.

Maintaining a strong community is an extremely important part of Judaism. Observing Shabbat every week helps keep the Jewish community connected and strong. It is a time to be with family, to socialise and relax, and to worship with other Jews in the synagogue. Some Jews also dedicate time to studying the Torah during Shabbat.

Hasidic Jews walking to the synagogue on a Saturday.

Shabbat at home

Before Shabbat, the family home is usually cleaned and tided. Sometimes flowers are put on display. All food is prepared before sunset on Friday because cooking is considered work. On the Friday evening, Jewish families have a special meal together. This begins with the father saying a special blessing over a cup of wine, called a Kiddush blessing. Kiddush means 'making holy'. The Kiddush cup is then passed around the table. Two portions of a special bread, called challah, are eaten at Shabbat meal. Before being eaten, the bread is blessed. At the end of Shabbat, blessings are recited over wine, spices and a candle.

Shabbat in the synagogue

There are usually two services in the synagogue during Shabbat. One is at sunset on the Friday; the other is on Saturday morning. Some Jews will attend both; others will attend one. The Saturday service can last up to two hours.

The challah bread reminds Jews of the food that God provided when they were in the desert during the Exodus.

A variety of things happen during this service. The first part of the Shema is recited as the Torah is removed from the Ark. The Torah is then read by someone from the bimah. In Reform synagogues, it is read in people's first language as well as Hebrew. The Torah is then returned to the Ark and a sermon is given by the rabbi (again in the language of the congregation). Following this, more prayers are said, including the 'Aleinu', which reminds Jews that it is their duty to praise God: 'Let us now praise the Sovereign of the universe and proclaim the greatness of the Creator...' This is followed by a prayer called the Kaddish, which says: 'Exalted and hallowed be God's great name, in the world which God created according to plan.' The service concludes with singing a hymn to God called 'Master of the World'.

Activity

Imagine you have spent Shabbat with a Jewish family. Describe what happened during the course of Shabbat.

Shabbat times on a smart phone.

Key vocabulary

Shabbat/Sabbath A day of rest and religious observance

Check your understanding

1. When do Jews observe Shabbat?
2. What are the origins of Shabbat?
3. How do Jews define work? Give examples of what might be considered work.
4. Why do you think it might be hard for Jews to observe Shabbat in the modern world?
5. 'All Jews should observe Shabbat.' Discuss this statement.

Unit 2: Judaism in the modern world
Jewish festivals

Festivals are an important part of Jewish life. What are the main Jewish festivals and what happens at them?

Rosh Hashanah

The dates of Jewish festivals are based on a lunar calendar, so they change each year. The first day of the Jewish year is called Rosh Hashanah, which means 'head of the year'. The Mishnah says that on Rosh Hashanah God writes down a person's actions, good and bad, and makes decisions about what sort of year he or she will have. God finalises this judgement on Yom Kippur, which comes 10 days later. This means that between Rosh Hashanah and Yom Kippur Jews spend time thinking about their behaviour, reflecting on their actions of the past year and making peace with others.

After visiting the synagogue, Jews wish one another 'L'shanah tovah' (a good year) before returning home to celebrate with a special meal. This includes extra fruit to symbolise renewal and the hope of a 'sweet' new year. Many Jews dip apple in honey, and pomegranate is often eaten to symbolise that people's good deeds should be as plentiful as pomegranate seeds.

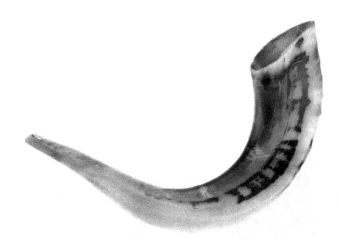

Many Jews return to the synagogue the next morning, where an instrument called a shofar is blown 100 times. The horn is meant to remind Jews of the ram that Abraham sacrificed instead of Isaac and that God will judge them for their actions. A ceremony called Tashlikh usually takes place in the afternoon, often near a stream or river. Jews empty their pockets to symbolise getting rid of sin.

A shofar is an ancient instrument made from a ram's horn.

Yom Kippur (Day of Atonement)

The holiest day of the year for Jews is Yom Kippur. It is a serious but joyful day because it offers Jewish people the chance to seek forgiveness from God and repair their relationship with him. Confessing wrongdoing is important, because Yom Kippur is the day on which God makes his final decision about what sort of year people have ahead of them. Many Jews fast for 25 hours. This is a mitzvah, and many Jews participate in order to build self-control or focus their mind. A large part of the day is spent praying in the synagogue. White clothes are often worn as a sign of purity. At the evening service, the Kol Nidre prayer is said, in which Jews cancel any promises made to God that they know they know they cannot keep.

Pesach (Passover)

At Pesach, Jews remember the night when the angel of death passed over Egypt, killing the firstborn sons of the Egyptians but sparing the Israelite boys. This was the tenth plague that God sent to the Egyptians, who were keeping the Israelites as slaves. After this plague, the Pharaoh agreed to let the Israelites go, and Moses led them out of Egypt. This story reminds Jews of God's power and their covenant with him.

Before Pesach begins, Jews remove any products containing yeast or leaven (the substance that makes bread rise) from their homes. This is because the slaves who rushed to escape Egypt did not have time to collect any yeast to make their bread rise, so they escaped with flat bread (matzot). This is the only type of bread eaten by Jews during Pesach.

The Seder plate.

The most important part of Pesach is the **Seder meal**. All the food at this meal has a symbolic meaning and helps Jews remember the difficulties of their ancestors. For example, bitter herbs represent the bitterness of slavery. A green vegetable dipped in salt water symbolises the tears of the slaves. A mixture of nuts, wine and apples called charoset is eaten to symbolise the cement that the slaves were forced to make for the Egyptians. There is also a roasted lamb shank bone, which is not eaten. This bone represents the lambs that were sacrificed in the Temple before it was destroyed. An egg is roasted as a symbol of new life, but this is also not eaten.

Matzot bread.

Seder wine

Four glasses of wine are drunk during the meal to remember God's four promises to Moses:

Say therefore to the people of Israel, 'I am the Lord and I will bring you out from captivity; I will welcome you with an outstretched arm; I will make you my people and I will be your God.

A fifth cup is poured and left for the prophet Elijah, who some Jews believe will return to announce the arrival of the Messiah at Passover. An empty chair will also be left for Elijah at the dinner table.

Key vocabulary

Seder meal A symbolic meal eaten at Pesach

Check your understanding

1 Why are festivals important for Jews?
2 What happens at Rosh Hashanah?
3 Why is Yom Kippur important to Jews?
4 Explain the symbolism of different items in the Seder meal.
5 'The Jewish festivals are all equally important.' Discuss this statement.

Birth, Bar Mitzvah and Bat Mitzvah

Important moments in the life of a Jew are marked by ancient rituals that are part of Jewish law. What are these moments and how are they honoured?

Birth

Jews believe that before a baby is born it has a soul, but its life does not begin until it has half emerged from its mother's body. When a baby is born it is sinless and pure. It is seen as a gift from God that should be celebrated.

In ancient times a woman had to spend time away from the Temple after giving birth. She was not permitted to touch anything sacred. This lasted for 40 days if the baby was a boy and 80 days if it was a girl, because the mother had created another creator. After this time, the woman would go to the Temple and make an offering to God. This ritual was based on the teachings of Leviticus 12 in the Torah. Today, a Jewish woman will have a mikvah (ritual bath) after a minimum period of 7 days if she has given birth to a boy and 14 days for a girl.

Circumcision

Circumcision is when a boy's foreskin is removed. This ceremony is performed when the baby is eight days old. In the past, fathers would often circumcise their sons, but today it is normally done by someone who is both religiously and medically qualified, called a **mohel**.

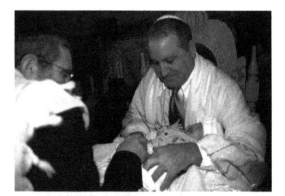

Circumcision is one of the most observed mitzvot. Even many secular Jews circumcise their sons. It is an ancient ritual, dating back to Abraham: God told the patriarch that he must circumcise himself and his descendants as a sign of God's everlasting covenant.

Circumcision of baby boys is practised in both Judaism and Islam, but it is a controversial issue in the modern world.

A father and his newborn son in a Jewish circumcision ceremony.

Some **atheists** argue that parents should not choose their son's religion before he is able to accept it for himself. They may also think it is wrong to make a permanent physical change to the body.

> ### Fact
>
> Many Jewish children are given two names. One is a Hebrew name; the other is a local name. A baby girl is given her names in the synagogue after her father has performed a special reading from the Torah. Boys are named after eight days, during their circumcision.

Bar Mitzvah and Bat Mitzvah

When boys and girls 'come of age' they have a ceremony called a **Bar Mitzvah** (boys) or **Bat Mitzvah** (girls). In Reform and Liberal communities, this happens at the age of 13. In Orthodox synagogues, girls usually have it a year earlier, at the age of 12. After the ceremonies, the young person is considered to be responsible for his or her own actions and faith. After the Bar Mitzvah, the boy can lead the synagogue service, can be included in a minyan or read from the Torah in the synagogue. In a Reform or Liberal synagogue, these rights would also be given to a girl after her Bat Mitzvah. After the ceremony, the boy will also begin to wear the tefillin in the synagogue. Some Liberal synagogues have a further service when the young person reaches 15 or 16, in which he or she confirms acceptance of the Jewish way of life.

For each ceremony, Jews are expected to study and prepare carefully, and they have to read certain texts. Most boys read from the Torah during their Bar Mitzvah, so they must have a basic understanding of Hebrew and how to read it. Girls will also spend time learning, volunteering and doing charitable tasks. Often their mother will teach them how to make challah bread for Shabbat. This emphasises the importance of the home to the Jewish way of life. In Reform and Liberal communities, it is common for boys to also be taught about jobs in the home, and girls will also read from the Torah at their Bat Mitzvah.

After the Bar or Bat Mitzvah ceremony has taken place in the synagogue, a special meal is shared. This is often followed by a celebratory event with family, friends and the synagogue community.

Fact

In Hebrew, Bar Mitzvah literally means 'son of the commandments' and Bat Mitzvah means 'daughter of the commandments'. There are references to the Bar Mitzvah in the Talmud, but the Bat Mitzvah has only been celebrated during the last century of Judaism.

Key vocabulary

atheist Someone who does not believe in God

Bar Mitzvah A ceremony for boys at the age of 13; it literally means 'son of the commandments'

Bat Mitzvah A ceremony for girls at the age of 12 or 13; it literally means 'daughter of the commandments'

mohel Someone who is both medically and religiously qualified to perform a circumcision

Check your understanding

1. What do Jews believe about newborn babies?
2. Describe what happened to the woman after giving birth in the times of the Temple and what happens today.
3. Why are Jewish boys circumcised?
4. Explain the key differences between Orthodox and Reform/Liberal Bar and Bat Mitzvahs.
5. 'The Bar/Bat Mitzvah is the most important moment in the life of a Jew.' Discuss this statement.

Marriage, funerals and mourning

What rituals do Jews perform during marriage and funeral ceremonies, and how do these help create a unique identity for Jews?

Marriage

The Torah does not provide Jews with much guidance about marriage. However, the Talmud explains how to find a partner, how a wedding ceremony should be conducted and how a husband and wife should treat each other. There are two stages to a Jewish marriage:

- kiddushin – the engagement between the couple
- nisuin – the full marriage.

A Jewish wedding ceremony usually lasts about half an hour. During the ceremony, the couple stands under a canopy called a **huppah**, which represents their new home together. The rabbi gives a talk, offering the couple a message about married life. The rabbi and guests also recite the **seven blessings** they hope that the couple will receive from God. In accordance with Jewish law, a plain metal ring is placed on the bride's right forefinger to show that the marriage has taken place.

In Orthodox ceremonies, the wedding and signing of the marriage contract has to be witnessed by two men. In other Jewish traditions, the witnesses can be men or women. After the signing of the contract, the groom stamps on a small glass as a reminder of the destruction of the Temple. After the ceremony, the couple retires to a room so they can spend some time alone before they re-join their family and friends for a meal and party.

The groom at a Jewish wedding ceremony sipping the wine which is blessed with the seven blessings.

Fact

In medieval times, some Jews believed in reincarnation – that your soul is reborn into another body after you die. Nowadays, Jews tend not to believe that souls are reincarnated.

Funerals

Some Reform and Liberal communities allow the bodies of dead people to be cremated, but, traditionally, the bodies of Jewish people are buried. In some countries, the body may simply be covered in a cloth, but in others Jews will usually use a very simple wooden coffin. If possible, the burial takes place within 24 hours of death, and the body is never left alone between the point at which a person dies and the burial. During this time, family members and friends pay respect to the person who has died. The body will be washed and wrapped in a shroud, and a tallit will be put on men. Some funerals take place in a synagogue, but others may be held at a funeral home or at the graveside. Services usually include readings, singing psalms and giving a **eulogy**.

Orthodox Jews paying respect at a Jewish funeral.

Mourning

When a loved one dies, people sometimes spend time mourning before returning to normal life. Mourning is an important part of Jewish life and this period follows five stages:

- Aninut – death to burial

- Shivah – the first seven days, starting on the day of burial

- Sheloshim – the first 30 days, starting on the day of burial and including the Shivah; this is the end of mourning, except when mourning for a parent

- Yud Bet Chodesh – the 'year of mourning' for a parent

- Yahrzeit – the anniversary of the death of the parent, according to the Jewish calendar

Orthodox Jewish prayer recited to honour the passing of a loved one, celebrate their life and help with coping during the mourning process.

Jews who are mourning might wear a torn black ribbon or a cut tie. This is because in the Torah, Jacob tore his clothes after hearing that his son Joseph had died. After the funeral, the mourners return home, and often share a meal of consolation. Stones are usually left at the grave rather than flowers. This is partly because stones are a permanent reminder and because stones were used to mark graves in the area where Judaism developed.

The seven days after the burial are a time for intense mourning during which Jews often stay at home, rejecting luxuries and fun activities. Special candles are lit and visitors will come to pay their respects, bringing food.

Life after death

Judaism focuses on this life rather than the next, so Jews have many different opinions about what happens after death. Some Jews speak about Olam Ha-Ba, which means 'the world to come', and Jews are generally convinced that death is not the end. Some believe there will be judgement and that those who follow God's commands will be welcomed to a place of spiritual perfection called Gan Eden; those who do not will go to **Gehinnom**, a place of purification. There is very little in the Tanakh about what happens when people die and most teaching about life after death comes from ancient rabbis.

Key vocabulary

eulogy A speech given in praise of someone who has just died

Gehinnom A place of purification in the afterlife

huppah A canopy which a couple stand under during their marriage ceremony to represent starting a new home together

seven blessings Blessings recited by the rabbi and others at a wedding ceremony

Check your understanding

1. What are the two stages to a Jewish marriage?
2. Outline what happens at a Jewish wedding ceremony.
3. Create a timeline of events from the death of a Jew to the end of mourning.
4. What do Jews believe about life after death?
5. 'It is better to focus on this life than what might happen next.' Discuss this statement, with reference to Judaism.

The value of human life

Obeying God's laws (mitzvot) is very important to Jews. What do Jews believe about human life?

Jews believe that the life of a human is more valuable than the life of any other living creature. They think that life should be respected because it is given by God and so is sacred. The Talmud states that everyone is descended from a single person, so harming or destroying one person is in some way like destroying the whole world.

What is Pikuach Nefesh?

Pikuach Nefesh is the idea that nearly any religious law can be broken in order to preserve human life. Jews believe that they should live by the Torah, but not die because of it. This means that if someone's life would be put in risk by fasting at Yom Kippur then the person should not fast. Equally, if someone is in danger of starvation, then it is acceptable to eat non-kosher food.

In the same way, it is acceptable to work on Shabbat if doing so will save someone's life. For example, doctors are allowed to answer emergency calls, and people can travel to hospitals in an emergency, even though driving is usually considered work. The principle of Pikuach Nefesh does not simply allow people to break laws – it actually requires that laws are broken in some situations. Leviticus 19.16 says 'You shall not stand aside while your fellow's blood is shed' and the Talmud says 'The Sabbath has been given to you, not you to the Sabbath.'

However, there are exceptions to the principle of Pikuach Nefesh. For example, adultery, murder, idolatry, denying God exists or using his name in vain should never be committed in order to save a life. Also, people should not put their own life in more danger than the person whose life they are trying to save.

Mount Sinai Hospital in the USA has a specially designed 'Shabbat elevator' that stops on every floor so that people observing Shabbat do not have to push a button in the lift, which would count as work.

Medical issues

The principle of Pikuach Nefesh also affects Jewish attitudes to abortion. Jews believe that if a pregnant woman is going to die, but having an abortion would save her life, then the foetus should be aborted. This is because her life is superior to the life of the foetus, which is not yet a human. Jews may think that it is acceptable to switch off life-support machines, but generally they think it is wrong to do anything that will bring about death.

One way in which people can help save lives is through donating their organs after they die. Liberal and Reform Jews usually allow organ donation. However, Orthodox Jews do not always agree with this, because sometimes the organs need to be removed while the donor's heart is still beating, which could be seen as killing that person.

Tattoos and piercings

Recently, tattoos and piercings have become more popular in society, and whether or not these are permitted has caused controversy among Jews. Many Jews think that these are banned in the Torah, which says: 'Do not cut your bodies for the dead or put tattoo marks on yourselves' (Leviticus 19.28).

Jews believe that our bodies are created in the image of God and should be seen as a precious gift, loaned from him. This means they are not our personal property to do with as we like. Piercing is less controversial because there are stories of Jews who have pierced ears in the Tanakh. Many Jews argue that a piercing is not a permanent act, and if ears can be pierced it is hard to justify other piercings being banned.

A Jewish man with a star of David tattoo.

Interpreting the Torah

The Torah teaches that people should be held accountable for their actions. A famous verse says: 'A life for a life, an eye for an eye, a tooth for a tooth' (Exodus 21.24).

It is unlikely that Jews ever took this verse literally. Often, justice would have been gained through payment of money to make up for a crime. The Talmud makes it clear that the Torah should not be taken literally and that it can only be fully understood with the Talmud's commentary. Jews believe that when someone has hurt another person, he or she should recognise this and seek forgiveness from God.

Key vocabulary

Pikuach Nefesh The principle that nearly any religious law can be broken in order to preserve human life

Check your understanding

1. Why do Jews believe that human life is sacred?
2. What does the principle of Pikuach Nefesh require of Jews?
3. Describe some modern situations where the principle of Pikuach Nefesh might be used.
4. Discuss different Jewish approaches to organ donation, tattoos or piercings.
5. How might Jews respond to the claim that they need to follow the teaching 'an eye for an eye' by seeking revenge?

A persecuted people

Through history, Jews have suffered for their beliefs. How and why have Jews been persecuted?

Early persecution

Jews have been **persecuted** since the early days of their religion. The book of Exodus describes how Moses freed the descendants of Abraham, the Israelites, from slavery in Egypt. The Tanakh also describes how the Jews lived under the control of the Babylonians after they invaded Jerusalem in 586 BCE and destroyed the Temple (see page 14). In 167 BCE, all Jewish worship, festivals and sacrifice were banned by the rulers of a Greek empire that took control of the area in which most lived. They forced Jews to worship Greek gods. In 70 CE, the Jewish Temple was destroyed for a second time, this time by the Romans who believed in many gods and did not like Jewish monotheism. This event caused Jewish communities to begin to spread around the world in an event called the diaspora ('dispersion').

The massacre of Jews in Rhineland, 1096.

Middle Ages

During the Middle Ages, some Christians blamed Jews for the death of Jesus, and **anti-Semitism** became common in Europe. Many Jews were murdered or expelled from countries, especially around the time of the **Crusades**. For example, in 1190, there was a massacre of Jews in the English city of York. People had accused the Jews of using the blood of Christian children in their religious rituals. A Christian mob responded by burning Jews who had taken refuge in a castle tower. One hundred years after the massacre in York, all Jews were expelled from England – a ban that lasted until 1656.

Jews were also blamed for the Black Death, a plague that killed approximately 60 per cent of people in Europe during the Middle Ages. At this time, Jews were also persecuted in Spain, where thousands of Jewish people were executed between 1066 and 1492, when Jews were expelled. This was followed by significant persecution of Jews in Russia, Germany and the Middle East in particular in the 1800s.

The yellow badge issued to Jews by the Nazi government in Germany from 1941 to 1945.

The Holocaust

The most severe persecution of Jews took place in the twentieth century. In 1933, Adolf Hitler and his political party, the Nazis, came to power in Germany. Living conditions in Germany were very poor at this time and Hitler blamed this on Jews. He said that they were enemies of Germany and he wanted to destroy them in what was called the Final Solution, the name given by the Nazis to the mass extermination of Jews. Jews were confined to small areas in cities called ghettos and then taken to concentration camps. There, they were executed, usually in gas

66 If heaven was full of paper and the oceans full of ink, I could not express my pain. 99
A child survivor of Auschwitz, a concentration camp

chambers. The best-known concentration camp is Auschwitz, in Poland. It is estimated that six million of the nine million Jews living in Europe at the time were killed between 1933 and the end of the Second World War in 1945. This mass killing of Jewish people is usually known as the **Holocaust**. However, many Jews (and non-Jews) do not like this term because it originally referred to a burnt animal sacrifice. They use the word **Shoah**, which means calamity or catastrophe, instead.

Timeline of persecution in Nazi Germany

1935 – Signs forbidding Jews from swimming pools and public places are put up. The Nuremberg laws forbid Jews from voting or marrying a German and take away their German citizenship.

1939 – Jews are forced to live in ghettos and have their businesses taken away by the Nazis.

1942 – An event called the Wansee Conference finalises Nazi plans for the extermination of Jews in Europe.

1933 – Jewish business are boycotted; Jewish civil servants, lawyers and teachers lose their jobs. Schoolchildren are taught that Jews were racially inferior.

1938 – Jewish doctors are banned and Jewish children are banned from schools. On 9 and 10 November attacks on Jewish homes, businesses and synagogues take place. This event is called Kristallnacht (meaning 'Night of Broken Glass' in German).

1941 – Jews have to wear a star of David badge for identification. Many Jews in Russia are murdered by Nazi Einsatzgruppen ('task forces').

Anti-Semitism today

Anti-Semitism still exists in the UK and many other parts of the world today. It might take the form of online abuse, personal attacks or attacks on people's property. In the UK, a charity called the Campaign Against Anti-Semitism aims to educate people about anti-Semitism in the hope that it will be eliminated. Every year, on 27 January, Holocaust Memorial Day takes place so that people do not forget what happened.

Protestors in London challenging antisemitism by demanding zero-tolerance and greater action by the police and government.

Key vocabulary

anti-Semitism Persecution of Jewish people

Crusades A series of wars between Christians and Muslims

Holocaust The killing of six million Jews by Nazi Germany

persecution Discrimination against people because of their beliefs

Shoah Another term for the Holocaust, which means calamity or catastrophe

Check your understanding

1 What is meant by 'anti-Semitism'?
2 How were Jews persecuted in the Middle Ages?
3 How many Jews were killed in the Holocaust?
4 Create a timeline of Jewish persecution in Nazi Germany.
5 Does anti-Semitism still exist today?

Unit 2: Judaism in the modern world
Jewish responses to the Holocaust

Jews believe that God is all-powerful (omnipotent), all-loving (omnibenevolent) and all-knowing (omniscient). How does this present difficulties when considering issues such as the Holocaust?

The 'problem of evil'

Over the course of history, people have tried to understand how God and evil can both exist. If God knows everything, he knows evil exists. If God is all powerful, he has the power to stop evil. If God is all good, surely he wants to stop evil. The existence of evil suggests that either God does not exist, or that he is not all-loving, all-powerful and all-knowing. Since the Holocaust, Jews have thought and written much about this 'problem of evil'.

Richard Rubenstein

In 1960, a Jewish man called Richard Rubenstein wrote a book called *After Auschwitz*. In it he argued that after the horror of the Holocaust Jews could no longer believe that God is omnipotent, or that they are his chosen people. Rubenstein said that the covenant between God and Abraham had been destroyed. After the Holocaust, more Jews became secular Jews. They could not believe in God, but wanted to continue the practices and rituals of Judaism. Rubenstein still believed in God and did not think that people should become atheists, but he thought that God had no involvement in or impact on the world. He did think, though, that it was still valuable to live a Jewish life, because the rituals gave life meaning.

Richard Rubenstein.

Eliezer Berkovits

Eliezer Berkovits was an Orthodox Jewish rabbi who claimed that God was not responsible for the Holocaust. He argued that although God wanted to stop the suffering he could not do this without interfering with human **free will**. God had to allow extreme suffering and evil to happen because he had given freedom to human beings. Berkovits said that God had to 'hide his face' (**hester panim**) during the Holocaust. He argued that, rather than speaking about the absence of God during the Holocaust, people should consider the absence of humanity. Jews today should use their free will to have a renewed faith and desire to make the world a better and more peaceful place.

Emil Fackenheim

Emil Fackenheim was a rabbi who wrote in the 1940s. He argued that turning away from Judaism after the Holocaust was the equivalent of giving Hitler a victory – Hitler's aim had been to wipe Judaism from the face of the earth, and if Jews abandoned their religion then Hitler would have achieved his goal. Fackenheim claimed that Jews have a responsibility to unite and continue the Jewish family and faith. He said that this was the 614th mitzvah that Jews should follow.

Anne Frank

Anne Frank was a Jewish girl born in 1929. She and her family fled from Nazi Germany to Amsterdam in the Netherlands in order to avoid persecution. She and her family hid in an attic in Amsterdam for two years before being arrested and sent to a concentration camp, where she died of disease at the age of 15. While in hiding, she wrote a diary, which has since been translated into 67 languages and has sold over 30 million copies.

Who has allowed us to suffer so terribly up till now? It is God that has made us as we are, but it will be God, too, who will raise us up again. If we bear all this suffering and if there are still Jews left, when it is over, then Jews, instead of being doomed, will be held up as an example. Who knows, it might even be our religion from which the world and all peoples learn good, and for that reason and that reason alone do we have to suffer now.

Anne Frank

The Tanakh on suffering

The Tanakh does not give one clear explanation for why God allows suffering. The book of Job suggests that humans should not try to understand why some good people suffer. In this book, Job, the main character, is tested by God, who allows Satan to attack him. Job loses everything that is important to him, yet remains faithful to God. God blesses him with more than he had before as a reward for his loyalty.

Other traditional Jewish responses to the question of suffering include the idea that suffering is in some way beneficial and therefore not a bad thing. In the Tanakh, the prophet Isaiah is described as a *suffering servant*, and so some rabbis suggest that Jews suffer in order to pay for the wickedness of the rest of humanity.

Key vocabulary

free will The ability to choose how to act

hester panim The belief that God 'hid his face' during the Holocaust because he could not interfere with free will

Check your understanding

1. What is the 'problem of evil'?
2. How could the Tanakh help Jews understand why there is evil and suffering in the world?
3. Explain how one Jewish thinker responded to the Holocaust.
4. Who was Anne Frank and how did she try to understand the suffering of Jews during the Holocaust?
5. 'There is no satisfactory response to the problem of evil for Jews.' Discuss this statement.

What is Zionism?

How have Jews tried to create their own state and what difficulties have they faced?

At the end of the nineteenth century, Jews all over Europe were being persecuted. Some decided that the solution was to create their own Jewish state where they could practise their religion freely. This ambition was called **Zionism**. The Holocaust (see pages 40–41) led many Jews to believe that having their own land was not only desirable but necessary for the survival of the Jewish people.

Zionists thought about where they could establish their homeland and decided that they should return to Jerusalem and the area surrounding it. Their ancestors had fled from this region 2000 years earlier in order to avoid persecution from their Roman rulers. During their reign, the Romans changed the name of the area from Judea to Palestine.

The battle for land

Over the course of history, Jerusalem has had many rulers, including Jews, Christians and Muslims. In 1917, during the First World War, Britain captured Jerusalem from the Muslim Ottoman Empire, which had ruled the area for 400 years. The British government supported the idea of establishing a Jewish state in Palestine, and hundreds of thousands of Jews moved there. However, this caused great difficulties between the Jews and the **Palestinians** who were already living there.

In 1947, war broke out between the Jews and Palestinians, and in 1948 the **United Nations** (UN) decided to split Jerusalem in two. The eastern half was given to Jordan and the western half became part of the **State of Israel**, which was the first Jewish state to exist for 2000 years. This decision was controversial because neither side thought that the other should exist as a nation or rule over part of Jerusalem. Jerusalem was home to Jewish people's ancestors and was the location of the Temple, so it was very important. However, the city is also important for Muslims – it is the location of the Al-Aqsa Mosque and the Dome of the Rock, which, according to the Qur'an, is where the Prophet Muhammad ascended to the heavens from earth during an event called the Night Journey.

During the Six-Day War in 1967, the Jewish **Israelis** captured more land from the Jordanians, including eastern Jerusalem and a Palestinian area called the West Bank. Since then, violence between Israeli Jews and Palestinian Muslims has continued to escalate and attempts to create lasting peace have been unsuccessful. In 2007, an area of land called the

3150 BCE	Cananites
1006 BCE	Israelites (Jewish)
586 BCE	Hellenists (Greek)
37 BCE	Romans
348 AD	Byzantines (Christian)
638 AD	Early Muslim conquests
1099 AD	Crusaders (Christian)
1187 AD	Mamelukes and Ottomans
1917 AD	British (Christian)
1948 AD	State of Israel (Jewish)
Present	

This chart shows who ruled Jerusalem at various points in its history.

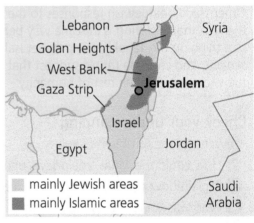

This map shows Israel and the surrounding area, with Jewish and Islamic areas highlighted.

Gaza Strip was returned to the Palestinians in an effort to improve the situation.

Israel today

Israel is a well-developed country with a population of about eight million people – 75 per cent of them are Jewish, 20 per cent are Muslim and five per cent are of other or no faith. This makes it the only place in the world with a majority Jewish population. Hebrew is the main language spoken. The capital is officially Jerusalem, though this is not recognised by many other countries. This is because they do not agree with the borders that Israel has put in place, which do not match the agreements made with the United Nations.

Anti-Zionist or anti-Semitic?

Anti-Zionism and anti-Semitism are not the same thing. Anti-Zionism means opposition to the existence of the Jewish state of Israel while anti-Semitism means hostility towards and prejudice against Jewish people. Some people argue that it is impossible to separate criticism of Zionism or Israeli politics from criticism of Judaism itself. Some even say that labelling someone a 'Zionist' is a form of abuse. Others claim that the Israeli government and its supporters deliberately confuse the definitions of Judaism with Zionism to try and stop people criticising their political decisions.

Key vocabulary

Israelis People who live in Israel; mainly Jewish

Palestinians People who live in and around the State of Israel; mainly Muslims

State of Israel A Jewish state set up by the United Nations in 1948, which has since expanded

United Nations An organisation set up after the Second World War to keep world peace

Zionism A Jewish movement that originally aimed to establish, and now aims to continue, the Jewish state of Israel

Controversy within Judaism

Zionism has always been a controversial issue within Judaism. A Holocaust survivor called Rabbi Joel Teitelbaum believed that Jews should wait for the Messiah to return them to the Promised Land and then set up a religious society there. He claimed that the Holocaust was God's punishment of the Jews for not waiting for the Messiah. Another Jewish thinker, Menachem Hartom, argued the opposite. He thought that the Holocaust was a punishment because Jews had fitted in to other cultures and not returned to the land God had given them. For other Jews, any suggestion that the Holocaust was God's punishment is seen as offensive. Former Chief Rabbi Jonathan Sacks wrote:

More than a million children were gassed, burned, shot, tortured or buried alive ... God forbid that we should add to their death the sin of saying that it was justified.

Jonathan Sacks, *Crisis and Covenant: Jewish Thought After the Holocaust* (Manchester University Press, 1992), p. 32

Check your understanding

1 Why did Jews want a country that could become their 'homeland'?
2 Why were the events of 1948 and 1967 controversial?
3 Describe what the country of Israel is like today.
4 Why might someone say that Zionism is an unhelpful term?
5 Explain why Zionism has been controversial within Judaism.

Unit 2: Judaism in the modern world
Knowledge organiser

Key facts

- Jews observe a day of rest each week, called Shabbat or the Sabbath. This is a day of rest on which they are not allowed to do any work.

- On Shabbat, many Jews will go to services at the synagogue. They also enjoy a special meal with family in which certain rituals are performed.

- The main Jewish festivals are Rosh Hashanah (the first day of the Jewish new year), Yom Kippur (the Day of Atonement) and Pesach (Passover).

- Jews observe certain rituals at significant moments in their lives. In ancient times, when a child was born, the mother would have to stay away from the Temple for 40 days for a boy and 80 days for a girl.

- Circumcision is a ritual in which a male's foreskin is removed, in remembrance of God's covenant with Abraham. This takes place when a boy is eight days old.

- Bar Mitzvah and Bat Mitzvah are ceremonies that mark a boy's or a girl's 'coming of age' at 13 years old. They must study carefully for these ceremonies and afterwards are considered to be responsible for their own actions and faith.

- The Jewish marriage is in two parts: the engagement and the full marriage. The ceremony is led by a rabbi who, along with the guests, recites the seven blessings for the couple.

- Jews are usually buried rather than cremated. Burial takes place within 24 hours of death if possible, and someone stays with the body the whole time until the burial.

- There are three stages to mourning after someone dies: Aninut, Shivah and Sheloshim. If a parent has died, there are two additional stages: Yud Bet Chodesh and Yahrzeit.

- Jewish law states that human life is sacred. Jews are allowed to break some of their laws if doing so will save someone's life. This principle is known as Pikuach Nefesh.

- Jews have been persecuted since ancient times. They have been expelled from countries where they were living many times, including from England in the 1200s.

- The worst case of Jewish persecution was at the hands of the German Nazis from 1933 to 1945. Millions of Jews were sent to concentration camps, where they were executed. This is known as the Holocaust or Shoah.

- The 'problem of evil' is the question of how God can allow terrible things such as the Holocaust to happen. If he is all-loving, all-powerful and all-knowing, he would prevent these events. Jews have different interpretations of and responses to the problem of evil.

- Zionism is a movement of re-establishment and development of a Jewish homeland in the area around Jerusalem. After the Second World War, Jews were allowed to return to Palestine, but this caused great conflict with the Palestinian people who were already living there. Difficulties continue in the region today, as Jewish Israelis and Muslim Palestinians both consider the region to be their homeland.

Key vocabulary

anti-Semitism Persecution of Jewish people

atheist Someone who does not believe in God

Bar Mitzvah A ceremony for boys at the age of 13; it literally means 'son of the commandments'

Bat Mitzvah A ceremony for girls at the age of 12 or 13; it literally means 'daughter of the commandments'

Crusades A series of wars between Christians and Muslims

eulogy A speech given in praise of someone who has just died

free will The ability to choose how to act

Gehinnom A place of purification in the afterlife

hester panim The belief that God 'hid his face' during the Holocaust because he could not interfere with free will

Holocaust The killing of six million Jews by hester Nazi Germany

huppah A canopy which a couple stand under during their marriage ceremony to represent starting a new home together

Israelis People who live in Israel; mainly Jewish

mohel Someone who is both medically and religiously qualified to perform a circumcision

Palestinians People who live in and around the State of Israel; mainly Muslims

persecution Discrimination against people because of their beliefs

Pikuach Nefesh The principle that nearly any religious law can be broken in order to preserve human life

pogrom An attack on Jews

Seder meal A symbolic meal eaten at Pesach

seven blessings Blessings recited by the rabbi and others at a wedding ceremony

Shabbat/Sabbath A day of rest and religious observance

Shoah Another term for the Holocaust, which means calamity or catastrophe

State of Israel A Jewish state set up by the United Nations in 1948, which has since expanded

United Nations An organisation set up after the Second World War to keep world peace

Zionism A Jewish movement originally aimed to establish, and now aims to continue, the Jewish state of Israel

Key people

Eliezer Berkovitz A rabbi who believed that God had to hide his face (hester panim) during the Holocaust so as not to interfere with human free will

Emil Fackenheim A rabbi who thought that the 614th mitzvah Jews should follow after the Holocaust was to unite and continue the Jewish family and faith so that Hitler did not win

Anne Frank A Jewish girl who wrote a diary while in hiding during the Holocaust

Richard Rubenstein A Jewish writer who claimed that Jews cannot think of God as omnipotent or that they are his chosen people after the Holocaust

A Jewish family at Shabbat.

Christianity

History and belief

In this book, you will find out about the most-followed religion in the world today – Christianity. In the first half of this book, you will discover how Christianity started, spread and split. You will find out how Christianity grew from a small group of people living in the Middle East 2000 years ago, to become a global religion followed by more than two billion people. You will explore how early Christians survived severe persecution, before the religion became a powerful force in the Roman Empire. You will also examine some of the major debates and disagreements among Christians that caused the religion to split into the many different forms of Christianity that exist today.

What is Christianity?

Today, there are 2.2 billion Christians around the world, making Christianity the most followed religion on the planet, but where did this religion come from and what do Christians believe?

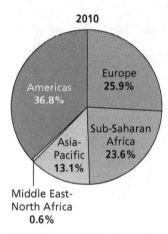

2010

Christian populations by region.

Where did Christianity begin?

Christianity began nearly 2000 years ago, in present-day Israel, which was then part of the Roman Empire. The first Christians had radical new beliefs. They claimed that a recently executed Jewish man named Jesus was the long-awaited Messiah. They believed that three days after being killed on a wooden cross Jesus had been **resurrected**. He appeared to many people before ascending to heaven. Christians claimed that Jesus had died so that people who believed in him could be forgiven for their sins and have eternal life.

These were extraordinary claims. They were very different from traditional Roman beliefs, as well as those of the Jews who lived in the Roman Empire at this time. Despite this, these early Christian beliefs spread rapidly across the Roman world, creating a new religion: Christianity.

What do Christians believe about God?

Christians are **monotheists**, which means that they believe in one God. However, Christians also believe that God is three. This distinctive belief – that God is both one and three – is called the **Trinity**. The three 'persons' of the Trinity are:

- God the Father (God in heaven)

- God the Son (Jesus)

- God the Holy Spirit (God in the world).

The **doctrine** of the Trinity is an attempt to express how Christians understand God. For 2000 years, Christians have tried to understand how it is possible for one God to be Father, Son and Holy Spirit at the same time. This belief has caused many disagreements, but, ultimately, Christians accept that God is a mystery and cannot be fully understood by humans.

Christians believe that God is the creator of the world and that he is eternal, which means that he has no beginning or end. They also think that he is omnipotent (all powerful), omniscient (all knowing) and omnibenevolent (all good). Christians believe that they can speak to God through prayer and they try to **worship** him through the way that they live.

> **Fact**
>
> At the time of Jesus, Jewish people were waiting for God to send them a Messiah – a rescuer or saviour. The word 'Messiah' is Hebrew and the Greek word for it is 'Christ'. People who believed that Jesus was the Messiah called him Jesus Christ, and so were given the name Christians.

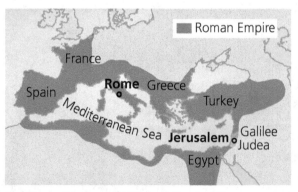

The Roman Empire at the time of Jesus's birth.

Denominations of Christianity

Christians are united by their faith in Jesus, but there is no such thing as a typical Christian. Over the past 200 years there have been many disagreements between Christians, and sometimes these have led to new types of Christianity. Today, there are over 30,000 **denominations** of Christianity. The largest of these is the Catholic Church.

The Bible

The Bible is a very important book for Christians. It teaches them about God and tells them how to live in a way that pleases him. The word 'Bible' comes from the Greek word *biblia*, meaning 'books'. The Bible contains many books, which are split into two sections: the Old Testament and the New Testament. Each book is divided into chapters and verses:

Book   Chapter   Verse

Genesis 1.27

Life after death

Christians believe that after people die they will be judged by God, based on their faith and how they have lived their lives. Most Christians think that some people will be rewarded in heaven and others will go to hell. However, Christians disagree about whether heaven and hell are real places, or whether they are metaphors or spiritual states of being that no one can fully understand.

Many Christians believe that the only way to get to heaven is by having faith in Jesus and following his teachings. One reason for this is that the Bible (John 3.16) says: 'God so loved the world that he gave his only Son so that whoever believes in him will not perish but have eternal life.' For these Christians, spreading the Christian message (**evangelism**) is an important part of their faith. Other Christians believe that an omnibenevolent God would not send somebody to hell for not believing in him, so they place less emphasis on evangelism.

Key vocabulary

denomination A group within Christianity

doctrine A belief held and taught by a particular denomination

evangelism Spreading the Christian message in order to convert people

monotheist someone who believes in one God

resurrected Brought back to life after dying

Trinity The belief that God is three as well as one – Father, Son and Holy Spirit

worship To show the highest respect or adoration for someone or something

Check your understanding
1 How many Christians are there in the world today?
2 What do Christians believe about Jesus?
3 Explain what Christians believe about God.
4 How is the Bible structured?
5 Explain different Christian beliefs about life after death and evangelism.

How did Christianity begin?

Spreading the Christian message could be dangerous work, as Paul found out, so how did Christianity grow at such an astonishing rate?

Christian followers

When Jesus lived on earth, he had 12 chosen followers called **disciples**. Yet within 20 years of his death, most major towns around the Mediterranean had a Christian community. Like the disciples, these Christians claimed that Jesus, the executed Jewish man, had been God living on earth. They said that he had risen from the dead and ascended to heaven, and that by believing in him their sins would be forgiven and they would have eternal life.

Within 100 years of Jesus's death, there were 300,000 Christians living across the Roman Empire. Most of them had never met Jesus and lived far away from his homeland. So how did the beliefs of a few Jewish men living in Israel become a global religion with 2.2 billion followers?

Paul's problems

In the years after Jesus's death, **missionaries** spread the Christian message throughout the Roman Empire. Life was tough for these travelling preachers. They often journeyed long distances and faced **persecution**.

One of these missionaries was a man named Paul, who spread the message about Jesus across Asia and Greece. Many people listened to him and became Christians, but the ideas he preached about also caused a lot of anger. Eventually, Paul was put in prison. He described his experiences in a letter written to Christians living in the city of Corinth. The full letter is in the New Testament.

> 66 [24]Five times I was given the thirty-nine lashes by the Jews; [25]three times I was whipped by the Romans; and once I was stoned. I have been in three shipwrecks, and once I spent twenty-four hours in the water. [26]In my many travels I have been in danger from floods and from robbers, in danger from my own people and from Gentiles; there have been dangers in the cities, dangers in the wilds, dangers on the high seas, and dangers from false friends. 99

> 66 [27]There has been work and toil; often I have gone without sleep; I have been hungry and thirsty; I have often been without enough food, shelter, or clothing. [28]And not to mention other things, every day I am under the pressure of my concern for all the churches. [29]When someone is weak, then I feel weak too; when someone is led into sin, I am filled with distress. 99

> 2 Corinthians 11.24–29

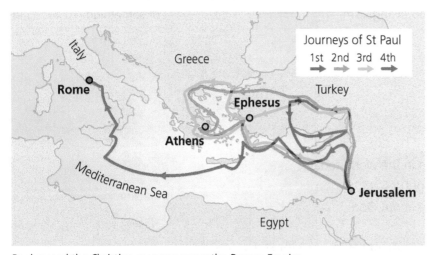

Paul spread the Christian message across the Roman Empire.

Who was Paul?

Before becoming a Christian, Paul was a passionate Jew who wanted to wipe out Christianity. One day, while travelling to the city of Damascus to persecute Christians, he saw a blinding light and heard the voice of God. He became a Christian and spent the rest of his life telling other people about Jesus. When the Jewish

Paul fooled the guards waiting at the gates of Damascus by escaping in a basket.

authorities realised Paul had converted to Christianity, they tried to kill him. Paul made a daring escape from the city by hiding in a basket while his supporters lowered him through a hole in the city walls.

The Council of Jerusalem

The early followers of Jesus were Jews who became Christians. As the Christian message spread through the Roman Empire, Jesus's followers faced a difficult question: should non-Jews (**gentiles**) also be allowed to follow Jesus? Paul met with leaders of Jesus's followers in Jerusalem to discuss this. At this 'Council of Jerusalem', they agreed that Jesus had died so that *all* people would be forgiven for their sins, not just Jews. Both Jews and gentiles could be followers of Jesus. They also agreed that non-Jewish people who became Christians did not need to undergo **circumcision**. In one of Paul's letters (Galatians 3.28), he wrote: 'There is no difference between Jews and gentiles, between slaves and free people, between men and women; you are all one in union with Christ Jesus.'

The decision to allow non-Jews to follow Jesus's teachings was momentous. Jesus's followers were no longer a group within Judaism. A new religion had begun, which needed a new name. The followers of Jesus became known as Christians because they believed that Jesus was the Christ.

Paul wrote many letters to the people who converted to Christianity on his travels.

Key vocabulary

circumcision The removal of a male's foreskin

disciples The 12 followers of Jesus who helped him to spread his message

gentiles A name given to non-Jews in the Bible

missionaries People who spread the Christian message

persecution Discrimination against a group of people

Check your understanding

1. What are missionaries?
2. List the difficulties Paul faced when spreading his message.
3. Before converting to Christianity, which religion did the first Christians follow?
4. What was decided at the Council of Jerusalem?
5. What sort of character was Paul? Give evidence to support your points.

What was life like for the Early Church?

Why was being a Christian so dangerous in the first three centuries and how did secrecy help the Early Church to survive?

Rumours in the Roman Empire

In CE 64, Nero was the Roman Emperor. During his reign a huge fire broke out and destroyed large parts of the city of Rome. Nero was an unpopular ruler. When he had a luxurious palace built in the place where the fire had destroyed other buildings, rumours spread that Nero had started the fire himself. However, Nero blamed Christians for the blaze. He gave orders that they should be rounded up and put to death. Some were set on fire and burned to death in the Roman arenas. Others were killed by vicious dogs.

Emperor Nero watching the burning of Christians.

Many people knew that Christians were not to blame for the fire in Rome, but they did not mind Christians being persecuted. Non-Christians believed that the **Early Church** was uncivilised and they did not understand its practices. One reason for this was that Christians met secretly at night. People heard that at these meetings Christians ate and drank the body and blood of Jesus, so they thought they were involved in cannibalistic feasts. In fact, the Christians were eating bread and drinking wine to remember Jesus's Last Supper and his death.

For the first three centuries, Christians were often persecuted. Under some emperors, they were persecuted if they refused to offer sacrifices to the gods that the Roman Emperor believed in. Many Romans thought that the success of the Roman Empire depended on keeping their gods happy, and they worried that the gods might be angered if the Christians did not respect them.

Pliny's letter to Emperor Trajan

Different parts of the huge Roman Empire were ruled by governors, acting on behalf of the Emperor. When there were problems in an area, governors would often blame Christians.

At the start of the second century, a Roman governor named Pliny was given a notebook filled with the names of Christians.

Christians sewn into wild animal skins and savaged to death by dogs during Emperor Nero's rule.

Pliny chose two Christian girls from this list and tortured them so they would give him information about what Christians believed and how they worshipped. This helped him devise a test. To find out if someone was a Christian, he made that person worship Roman gods, offer incense and wine to a statue of the Roman Emperor, Trajan, and deny following Jesus. If his prisoners did these things, they were freed. If they refused, they were executed as Christians.

Pliny was concerned by the growth of Christianity and wrote a letter to Emperor Trajan in CE 112. He said: 'The superstition has spread like the plague, not only in the cities but in the villages and the countryside as well. I feel it must be stopped and checked.'

Trajan wrote back to Pliny. He said that if somebody was accused and found guilty of being a Christian then that person should be killed, but that Christians should not be targeted and hunted down. Other emperors in the first three centuries were less tolerant. Although many Christians were **martyred** in the first three centuries, their deaths helped publicise Christianity, which continued to spread across the Roman Empire.

> 66 The blood of the martyrs is the seed of the Church. 99
> Tertullian, a Christian writer in the third century

Christians would bury bodies on the ledges of the catacombs.

Secret tunnels and tombs

In the first three centuries CE, people were often cremated (their bodies were burned) after death. Christians believed that they would be resurrected, so they wanted to be buried rather than cremated. They were not allowed to use land in Rome for their burials, so they used a 560-kilometre network of tunnels and caves beneath the city. These underground passages are known as the **catacombs**. There are 40 separate catacombs under Rome. In the largest, called Domitilla Catacombs, there are more than 14 kilometres of tunnels. You can still find bones and see a painting of the Last Supper that dates from the second century in these catacombs today.

Another advantage of the catacombs was that Christians could hide in them and hold meetings there during periods of persecution. The Roman authorities knew the catacombs existed and they probably knew that Christians were meeting there. However, Roman soldiers were not keen on going into – and perhaps getting lost in – dark tunnels filled with dead bodies!

Key vocabulary

catacombs Tunnels full of tombs underneath Rome

Early Church Christians in the first three centuries CE

martyred When someone is killed for their beliefs

Check your understanding

1 What did Emperor Nero blame on Christians in CE 64? What happened to the Christians?
2 What rumour was spread about Christian meetings?
3 Describe how Pliny and Trajan treated Christians.
4 Explain what the quote from Tertullian means.
5 Give three reasons why the Early Church used the catacombs.

Constantine and the Council of Nicea

Why did life change so dramatically for Christians after the conversion of Constantine and why did he call a meeting of bishops in Nicea in CE 325?

The conversion of Constantine

During the first three centuries of Christianity, Roman emperors either persecuted Christians or simply ignored them. The emperors themselves were not Christians. Roman authorities had been responsible for Jesus's execution, and emperors would not follow a religion that worshipped a Jewish criminal.

The Battle of Milvian Bridge, which Constantine believed he won with God's help.

This changed in CE 312. The Roman Emperor Constantine was preparing for a battle against his enemy, Maxentius. Rumours spread that Maxentius had help from magical powers, so Constantine was afraid that he was going to lose the battle. Constantine's mother was a Christian, so he decided to pray to her God for victory. Legend says that while Constantine was praying he looked up to the clouds and saw a bright cross bearing the words 'conquer by this'. The next day, Constantine sent his army into battle carrying a cross. His men defeated Maxentius' army. Constantine believed that the Christian God had granted him this victory, so he converted to Christianity.

Secret signs

Because of the threat of persecution, the Early Church often had to be secretive. They met in secret locations and they had secret signs. One of the most popular signs was a fish. The Greek word for fish is *ichthus*. Each letter stands for a different word in Greek:

I	Jesus
Ch	Christ
Th	God (Theos)
U	Son
S	Saviour

Secret Christian signs were engraved on walls, floors and objects all around the Roman Empire. They were a way for Christians to show devotion to God and communicate with each other.

The Edict of Milan

A year later, Constantine passed the Edict of Milan. This made Christianity legal and allowed Christians to meet and worship freely, without fear of persecution. The edict also banned Jews from owning Christian slaves. Constantine ordered that any property that had been taken from Christians must be returned to them. He even gave his wife's palace to the **Bishop** of Rome.

Constantine ordered more copies of Christian **scriptures** to be made and more churches to be built. Christians were now offered good jobs and given privileged treatment in court. Church leaders were not required to pay certain taxes. In CE 321, Sunday was declared an official Christian day of rest, when markets and workplaces were closed. Within 100 years of Constantine's conversion, Christianity had become the main religion in the Roman Empire.

The Council of Nicea

Constantine had ended the persecution of Christians, but the Church's troubles were not over. A man named Arius began causing arguments in the Christian community by raising questions about the identity of Jesus. Arius claimed that God had created Jesus, so Jesus must be a lesser being than God. This is known as the 'Arian controversy'.

Arius's ideas were becoming popular and Constantine was afraid that they might split the Christian Church and the Roman Empire. In CE 325, he called a meeting of 220 bishops, which took place at Nicea (in modern Turkey), to discuss the Arian controversy and to agree exactly what relationship Jesus had to God.

The bishops at the Council of Nicea agreed that Arius's ideas were **heresy**. They wrote a **creed**, known as the Nicene Creed, outlining the beliefs that all Christians should hold. The creed stated that Jesus is 'true God' and 'of one substance with the Father'. The creed is still recited in church services around the world today.

Constantine presides over the First Council of Nicea.

Key vocabulary

baptism A ritual in which people are immersed in water to symbolise turning away from sin and following God

bishop A Christian leader with authority over the priests and churches in an area

creed A statement of belief

heresy Beliefs that are opposed to those of the Church

scriptures Religious texts, such as the Bible

Check your understanding

1. Why did the Early Church use signs? Explain the meaning of a popular sign used.
2. Why was Christianity unappealing for Roman emperors in the first three centuries?
3. Why did Constantine convert to Christianity?
4. Make a table showing what life was like for Christians before and after Constantine's conversion.
5. What was the Arian controversy and how was it settled?

The Great Schism and the Catholic Church

Why did the Church in the East split from the Church in the West in 1054 and how do Catholic beliefs differ from those of other denominations?

The Bishop of Rome

When Christianity began, Rome was the most important city in the Roman Empire, so the Bishop of Rome was effectively in charge of the whole Church. As Rome declined in importance, however, there was less reason for the Bishop of Rome to have greater powers than other bishops.

In CE 440, the Bishop of Rome was a man named Leo. Leo did not want to lose his power and influence, so he said that before Jesus ascended to heaven he had put his disciple Peter in charge of the whole Church. Leo claimed that Peter was the first Bishop of Rome and that the authority given to Peter by Jesus was passed from one Bishop of Rome to the next.

For many centuries, people accepted this decision, but by 1054 Christians in the East no longer wanted to be led by the Bishop of Rome (whom we now call the Pope). In addition, Christians in the West wanted to change the wording of the Nicene Creed. Christians in the East did not want this. These disagreements led to the 'Great Schism' – a split in the Church. The Church in the East became known as the Eastern Orthodox Church and the Church in the West became the Catholic Church.

The Catholic Church

Today, approximately half of Christians follow Catholicism. Catholics have some beliefs that other Christians do not share.

Pope Leo I suggested that whoever held the title of Bishop of Rome would also be leader of the Christian Church.

Transubstantiation

Christians often have Holy Communion services at church, where they eat bread and drink wine to remember Jesus's death. This is known as the **Eucharist**. Catholics, however, believe that when the priest repeats Jesus's words from the Last Supper, the bread and wine actually turn into the body and blood of Jesus (although their outward appearance stays the same). This is called **transubstantiation**. Other Christian denominations think that the bread and wine symbolise Jesus's body and blood, but are not transformed.

Confession

In order to be forgiven for their sins, Catholics go to confession. They sit either face to face with a priest or in a **confessional** and explain how they have sinned. In a confessional, they are separated by a wall with a grid or curtain in it so that the priest and the person confessing cannot see each other.

A traditional confessional.

If someone is genuinely sorry for what he or she has done and wants to change, the priest will give the person **penance**. Priests must never reveal what people tell them in confession.

There is often a statue of Mary in Catholic churches.

Fact

In Catholic churches, the communion service is known as Mass. Often, the priest drinks any wine left over from the Eucharist. This is because they believe that it is Jesus's blood, so it should not be wasted.

Holy water

Near the entrance in Catholic churches there is often a small bowl of water that has been blessed by a priest. Catholics dip two fingers in the water and make the sign of a cross. They do this by moving their hand from their forehead to their chest and then from their left shoulder to their right shoulder. While doing this, Catholics usually say 'In the name of the Father, and of the Son and of the Holy Spirit' to express their belief in the Trinity and to remind them of their baptism.

Purgatory

Most Christians believe in heaven and hell. Catholics also believe in purgatory, which is not mentioned in the Bible. Catholics believe that purgatory is where souls are purified before going to heaven. A soul cannot go from purgatory to hell. By praying for a dead person's soul, Catholics believe that they can speed the passage from purgatory to heaven.

The Virgin Mary

Catholics place greater importance on Jesus's mother, Mary, than many other Christian denominations. They believe that unlike all other humans Mary was born into the world without sin. Catholics believe that when Mary died her body and soul were taken to heaven. They pray to Mary because they believe that she will act on their behalf before God when they reach heaven.

Activity

Divide your page into four boxes. In each box draw an image that represents a Catholic belief and explain the belief.

Key vocabulary

confessional A booth where Catholics ask a priest to grant them God's forgiveness

Eucharist The practice of eating bread and drinking wine during a church service

penance Prayer or some other action to show that one is sorry for sinning

transubstantiation The belief that the bread and wine become the actual body and blood of Jesus during the Eucharist

Check your understanding
1 What was the Great Schism and why did it happen?
2 What do Catholics believe happens during the Eucharist?
3 How do Catholics receive forgiveness for their sins?
4 How do Catholic beliefs about life after death differ from those of other Christians?
5 Why is Mary important in Catholicism?

Who is the Pope?

There are about 1.1 billion Catholics in the world, so the head of the Catholic Church, the Pope, is an extremely influential figure. How is he chosen?

From Peter to Francis

Catholics believe that the Pope is a successor of the disciple Peter, whom Jesus put in charge of the Church. The Pope lives in the world's smallest country, Vatican City, which is located in Rome. Popes can come from anywhere in the world, but there has only ever been one British Pope – Adrian IV, who was chosen in 1154. The current Pope, Francis, is from Argentina and is the first non-European to hold this office for more than 1300 years.

Francis is the 266th pope.

> ### Fact
> When someone becomes Pope, he chooses a new name for himself. The name shows people what issues the Pope feels are important and whose example he might follow. Pope Francis named himself after the twelfth-century Saint Francis of Assisi, who was very concerned about the poor and caring for the natural world.

Secrecy and smoke

After the Pope, the most senior leaders in the Catholic Church are **cardinals**. They are sometimes called 'Princes of the Church'. There are over 200 cardinals, from different countries.

Catholics believe that the Pope is chosen by God through a meeting of cardinals called a **conclave**. This is a highly secretive process. All cardinals who are under 80 years old meet in Vatican City to discuss which of them will be the next pope. They are not allowed any contact with the outside world during this time. All newspapers, TV, radio, internet and mobile phones are banned.

After the discussion, a secret vote is held in the Sistine Chapel. A cardinal needs two-thirds of all the votes to become Pope, so sometimes there are several rounds of voting. After each vote, the ballot papers are read and then burned, giving off black smoke from the chimney of the Sistine Chapel.

Catholics believe that the Holy Spirit guides the conclave.

When a new pope has been chosen, chemicals are added to the papers, causing the smoke to turn white. A bell is also rung from St Peter's Basilica.

During this process, huge numbers of Catholics from all over the world gather in Vatican City to wait for the announcement. The only clue they have about what is happening inside is the smoke and bell. Once the Pope is appointed, he makes his first public appearance. He usually makes a short speech and gives a blessing to the waiting crowds.

The first conclave

The first conclave took place in 1268. Local villagers had become angry at how long it was taking the cardinals to choose the new Pope, so they locked them in the palace. To encourage the cardinals to make a decision, the villagers tore the roof off the palace and gave them only bread and water to eat and drink. The conclave lasted nearly three years and three of the twenty cardinals died while it was happening.

The Pope and the public

In 1981, someone tried to assassinate Pope John Paul II. Since then, popes have usually travelled in a bullet-proof vehicle nicknamed the 'Popemobile'. However, Pope Francis prefers not to travel in the Popemobile because he feels that it separates him from people. He has also chosen not to live in the palace where the Pope traditionally lives. Instead, he lives in a small flat that is normally used by guests who are visiting the Pope.

The bullet-proof glass in the Popemobile keeps the Pope safe while he is out in public.

On the Thursday before Easter Sunday – Maundy Thursday – it is traditional for the Pope to wash and kiss twelve chosen people's feet. This is a re-enactment of Jesus's washing of his disciples' feet, as recorded in the New Testament. In 2015, Pope Francis broke with tradition by doing this in a prison. In 2016, he became the first Pope to include women and Muslims in this ritual, which took place at a refugee centre.

Activity

Imagine you are a newspaper reporter in Vatican City on the day that Pope Francis is elected. Describe the atmosphere, what is happening, how the Catholic crowds are feeling and why it is an important day for them.

Key vocabulary

cardinals The most senior members of the Catholic Church, after the Pope

conclave The meeting at which a new pope is elected

Pope Francis kissing a prisoner's feet.

Check your understanding

1. How many Catholics are there in the world?
2. What do Catholics believe about the Pope?
3. Explain in detail how the Pope is chosen.
4. What is the significance of Pope Francis's name?
5. Explain three ways in which Pope Francis has broken with tradition.

The Reformation and the Salvation Army

For 450 years after the Great Schism, the Church in the West was united, so why did a movement known as the Reformation lead to a split in Western Christianity in the sixteenth century?

Martin Luther and the Reformation

One of the leaders of the **Reformation** was Martin Luther, a German monk. He believed that the Catholic Church had strayed from the teachings of the Bible. To draw attention to this issue, in 1517 he nailed a list of 95 theses (complaints) to the door of his church in the town of Wittenberg.

A common Church practice at this time was the sale of **indulgences**. People paid the Church money and in return they were told they would spend less time in purgatory. Luther thought this was wrong. He believed that people could pray to God directly for forgiveness – they should not have to buy it from their priest. Luther also taught that the Bible, rather than the Pope, should be the greatest source of guidance for Christians. Any rule or teaching that was not in the Bible did not need to be followed, even if the Pope said it should.

During Church services, the Bible was always read in Latin. Luther and other reformers translated the Bible into their own language (German). This meant that people no longer had to rely on a priest to tell them what the Bible said. They could read it for themselves.

Martin Luther nailing his 95 theses to a church door in Wittenberg, Germany.

As these ideas took hold, Luther began to be seen as a threat to the power of the Pope and the Catholic Church. The Pope issued a document accusing Luther of heresy – going against official Church teachings – but Luther simply burned it. In response, the Pope **excommunicated** Luther. Despite this, Luther's ideas continued to spread. New Churches were created based on his teachings. They were known as **Protestant** churches because they protested against the ideas of the Catholic Church.

The Church of England

At this time, the King of England, Henry VIII, no longer wanted to be married to his wife, Catherine of Aragon. The only person who could allow them to separate was the Pope, but the Pope refused. In response, Henry broke with the Catholic Church and made himself head of the new Church of England in 1534. Later, the Church of England, also known as the Anglican Church, became the country's official religion, and it remains so today.

Henry VIII is shown here exerting his authority over the Roman Catholic Church. The Pope lies under the king's feet.

The Salvation Army

In the centuries following the Reformation, many other Protestant denominations were established. In 1865, William Booth set up the Salvation Army. He believed that churches in England only attracted wealthy middle-class people. Booth wanted a denomination that appealed to poor and working-class people. For this to work, he believed that the Church should take its message to the people rather than waiting for them to come to church. Booth and others who joined the Salvation Army went to the poorest parts of British cities to preach about Jesus. This was dangerous work: in 1882 alone, more than 600 members of the Salvation Army were physically assaulted.

A musical movement

William Booth is supposed to have once said: 'Why should the devil have all the best tunes?' In the nineteenth century, the Salvation Army became well known for taking popular tunes and putting Christian lyrics to them. On early missions, this helped drown out any abuse being shouted at members, and helped diffuse tension. Music remains important to the denomination and today there are about 2500 Salvation Army brass bands worldwide.

By the mid-1880s, the Salvation Army had decided to take a different approach. Its leaders thought that the poor would be more willing to listen to their message if they were offered food and shelter. The Salvation Army still follows this practice today. Every night, it provides more than 3000 homeless people with a bed in one of its 50 shelters. It also works with prisoners and helps people with addictions. Today, there are 1.5 million members of the Salvation Army in more than 100 different countries, including approximately 50,000 in the UK.

Fact

Like a military army, there are officers in the Salvation Army who wear a uniform. Members sometimes also choose to wear uniform, but this is not a requirement.

Key vocabulary

excommunicated Expelled from the Church

indulgences Certificates that people bought from the Catholic Church so they would spend less time in purgatory when they died

Protestant A form of Christianity that began in the sixteenth century as a protest against the Catholic Church

Reformation A sixteenth-century movement to reform the Church, resulting in the division of the Western Church into Catholicism and Protestantism

Check your understanding
1 Who was Martin Luther and why was he unhappy with the Catholic Church?
2 What was the result of Martin Luther's protests?
3 What did Henry VIII do and why?
4 How did people react to the Salvation Army in its early years?
5 Describe how the Salvation Army helps people in need today.

Quakers and the Amish

Christianity is a diverse religion. The many different denominations have very different beliefs and practices, as the Society of Friends and the Amish show, but what do these two denominations believe and how do they live?

The Society of Friends

The Society of Friends was established in 1650 by the Englishman George Fox, who thought Christians should return to the pure beliefs and simple lifestyle of the Early Church. He chose this name because he wanted followers to be friends with one another and with Jesus. Today, there are around 210,000 members around the world, including 17,000 in Britain. They are commonly known as 'Quakers'.

Quakers gather in meeting houses rather than in churches. The rooms in meeting houses are plain and simple. Members sit silently in a circle or a square, usually for an hour. The silence is only broken if someone feels that the Holy Spirit is leading him or her to say something. He or she might read a passage from the Bible or another book, or pray, or speak about an experience that he or she has had. Discussions and arguments are not allowed during the meeting and there is always a period of silence after someone has spoken. This allows others to reflect on what has been said. The meetings do not follow any fixed structure and sometimes nobody will speak for the whole hour.

> **Fact**
>
> The name 'Quakers' dates from the year the Society of Friends began, when George Fox told two local magistrates that they should 'tremble at the word of the Lord'.

Although Quakers have meeting houses, they believe that their meetings can take place anywhere.

In Quaker meetings there is no leader, no music and no creeds. Quakers believe that these things can be an obstacle to experiencing God directly. Quakers think that faith is personal and should not rely on someone else's ideas or words. They place less emphasis on the Bible than other Protestant denominations, because they believe that people should find spiritual truth in their own experiences and let their consciences guide their moral decisions.

> **Activity**
>
> Create a detailed spider diagram showing what happens in a Quaker meeting and explaining why.

The Amish

There are approximately 200,000 Amish Christians living across the USA. They live in small rural communities and keep themselves separate from the world. Their faith is strongly influenced by the Bible, in particular Romans 12.2: 'Do not be conformed to this world.' Each Amish community has slightly different rules, but they have many beliefs and practices in common.

Technology

The Amish have no electricity in their homes, and no technology such as televisions, radios or computers. They feel that technology can damage the community. There may be one telephone box that all families share, but they do not have phones in their homes as this would connect them to the outside world. However, because Amish men are often farmers, some communities do allow the use of tractors.

Amish are allowed to travel in someone else's car, but they do not own cars, using horse-drawn buggies instead.

Family and children

The Amish do not try and convert people and they marry within their community, so it is difficult for outsiders to join the Amish. However, their numbers are increasing. This is because they do not believe in contraception, so they often have large families.

Amish children go to Amish schools until they are 14. They are then trained in practical work. Most Amish communities allow young people to leave for a few years at the age of about 16 in order to experience life outside. At the end of this time they must decide whether to return to the Amish community and be fully baptised, or leave permanently. Between 85 and 90 per cent of young people choose to return.

Amish girls in traditional clothing.

Clothes

Amish women make most of their family's clothes. Women dress modestly, in long-sleeved dresses, aprons and bonnets, and wear no makeup. Men usually wear straw hats, plain trousers and shirts without stripes or patterns.

Church

Sunday is a day of rest when the Amish focus on their family and on spiritual matters rather than work. There are no church buildings; instead, people take it in turns to host the church service at their house. These services can last up to three hours and are followed by a meal together. Services are held in a German dialect, which is the language that the Amish people use to communicate with each other.

> **Fact**
>
> If someone breaks the rules of the Amish community, they are excommunicated. Remaining members are allowed to talk with excommunicated members, but they cannot eat or travel with them.

Check your understanding

1. What happens at a Quaker meeting?
2. Why do Quakers not use music and creeds in their meetings?
3. Why do Amish people not have technology in their homes?
4. How do church services work in Amish communities?
5. Explain five ways in which Amish life is different from your own life.

Unit 1: History and belief
Knowledge organiser

Key vocabulary

baptism A ritual in which people are immersed in water to symbolise turning away from sin and following God

bishop A Christian leader with authority over the priests and churches in an area

cardinals The most senior members of the Catholic Church, after the Pope

catacombs Tunnels full of tombs underneath Rome

circumcision The removal of a male's foreskin

conclave The meeting at which a new pope is elected

confessional A booth where Catholics ask a priest to grant them God's forgiveness

creed A statement of belief

denomination A group within Christianity

disciples 12 men that Jesus chose to be his followers

doctrine A belief held and taught by a particular denomination

Early Church Christians in the first three centuries CE

Eucharist The practice of eating bread and drinking wine during a church service

evangelism Spreading the Christian message in order to convert people

excommunicated Expelled from the Church

gentiles A name given to non-Jews in the Bible

heresy Beliefs that are opposed to those of the Church

indulgences Certificates that people bought from the Church so they would spend less time in purgatory when they died

martyred When someone is killed for their beliefs

missionaries People who spread the Christian message

monotheist someone who believes in one God

penance Prayer or some other action to show that one is sorry for sinning

persecution Discrimination against a group of people

Protestant A form of Christianity that began in the sixteenth century as a protest against the Catholic Church

Reformation A movement to reform the Church resulting in the division of the Western Church into Catholicism and Protestantism

resurrected Brought back to life after dying

scriptures Religious texts, such as the Bible

transubstantiation The belief that the bread and wine become the actual body and blood of Jesus during the Eucharist

Trinity The belief that God is three as well as one – Father, Son and Holy Spirit

worship To show the highest respect or adoration for someone or something

A stained glass window showing the crucifixion of Jesus.

Key facts

- Christianity began in present-day Israel nearly 2000 years ago. It began with the belief that Jesus had died to forgive people's sins and was resurrected from the dead so that all people could have eternal life.

- The message of Christianity was spread around the Roman Empire by missionaries such as Paul.

- Christianity developed out of Judaism, but at the Council of Jerusalem it was decided that both gentiles – non-Jews – and Jews could become Christians.

- Members of the Early Church were persecuted and martyred until the Roman Emperor Constantine passed the Edict of Milan in CE 313, following his conversion to Christianity after winning the Battle of Milvian Bridge in CE 312.

- Christians are monotheists who believe in the Trinity – God the Father, Son and Holy Spirit. In CE 325, at the Council of Nicea, bishops wrote the Nicene Creed. This stated that Jesus is fully God.

- In 1054, the Church in the East split from the Church in the West. This is called the 'Great Schism'. The Church in the East became known as the Eastern Orthodox Church and the Church in the West became the Catholic Church.

- In 1517, a German monk called Martin Luther nailed his 95 theses to a church door in Wittenberg, sparking the Protestant Reformation, which split the Western Church. In 1534, Henry VIII established the Church of England.

- There are over 2.2 billion Christians in the world today who belong to one of the 30,000+ denominations of Christianity. These include the Salvation Army, Society of Friends (Quakers) and the Amish.

- The largest denomination of Christianity is Catholicism. Catholics believe in transubstantiation, purgatory, confession and the importance of Mary, the mother of Jesus. The leader of the Catholic Church is the Pope. He is elected by cardinals at a meeting called a conclave.

Martin Luther, the German monk who led the Reformation.

Key people

Arius A heretic (someone who has committed heresy) whose ideas were condemned at the Council of Nicea

William Booth The founder of the Salvation Army

Constantine A Roman emperor who converted to Christianity in CE 312

Emperor Nero The Roman emperor during the fire in Rome in CE 64

Emperor Trajan A Roman emperor who wrote to Pliny with advice on dealing with Christians

George Fox English founder of the Society of Friends or Quakers in 1650

Henry VIII The King of England who founded the Church of England in 1534

Jesus A Jewish man, believed by Christians to be the Messiah and Son of God

Martin Luther A German monk who led the Reformation

Mary The mother of Jesus, she is especially important to Roman Catholics

Paul A travelling preacher and author of letters in the New Testament

Peter Jesus's disciple, whom Catholics believe was the first Bishop of Rome

Pliny A Roman governor who persecuted early Christians

Pope Francis The current Pope

Pope Leo I The Pope who in CE 440 said that the Bishop of Rome should lead the whole Church

Christianity in the modern world

The world today is very different from the way it was when Christianity began, and Christians on every continent now face challenges that people in the past did not have to consider. For example, over the past 300 years, Western peoples' ideas about religion, science and the roles of different genders have changed dramatically. In the second half of this book, you will consider how Christianity has responded to the challenges that these changes have brought.

Christianity has had a huge influence on our history and it has helped to shape the modern world. It has motivated people to create beautiful music, literature and art, but it has also played a part in slavery and wars. It has influenced emperors, kings and queens and shaped the laws of many nations. Yet, Christianity has been banned in other countries and, even today, there are places in the world where Christians are killed because of their beliefs. As you study more about Christianity in this chapter, you will gain a greater understanding of the past, the modern world and the lives of people around the world who call themselves Christian.

Unit 2: Christianity in the modern world
What is the Bible?

Throughout history, the Bible has been a source of inspiration for Christians, so why has it has also caused serious disagreements?

Who wrote the Bible?

The word Bible comes from the Greek word *biblia*, which means 'books'. This is because the Bible is not one book, but many. In the Protestant Bible, there are 66 books arranged into two sections: 39 are in the **Old Testament** and 27 are in the **New Testament**. In the Catholic Bible, there are 7 more books included in the Old Testament.

No one knows for sure who wrote some of the books or exactly how long ago they were written, but there seem to have been about 40 different authors who wrote over a period of many centuries. The Old Testament was written in the centuries before the birth of Jesus. It tells the story of a nation of people called the Israelites, who were God's chosen people. The Israelites later became known as Jews.

Most of the books in the New Testament were written within 70 years of Jesus's death. The first four books are about Jesus's life and are known as the **Gospels**. Nearly all the other books are letters written to early Christians. These letters still teach Christians today what to believe and how to live. The biblical authors did not know that their words would end up reaching such a wide audience. So how *did* their writings end up in the Bible?

Heresy was a constant threat to the unity of the Early Church, so it was important for Christians to agree on which religious writings were to be included in the Christian Bible. By the end of the fourth century, Christian leaders had largely agreed which books should be seen as **authoritative**.

The authors did not know that, centuries later, their writings would end up in the bestselling book that we call the Bible.

Ancient texts

The oldest surviving copies of parts of the New Testament date from the second and third centuries. The earliest complete copy of the Bible that exists was written in the middle of the fourth century. It is called the 'Codex Sinaiticus' and it is now in the British Library. In 1935, a short extract from John 18 was found in Egypt. In this chapter, *Pontius Pilate*, a Roman governor, questions Jesus before his crucifixion. Scholars have called it P52 and think it was written around CE 135, making it the oldest existing New Testament fragment.

The battle for the Bible

Throughout Christian history, the Bible has been at the heart of debates and disagreements among Christians. Some people have used it to support slavery, war and sexism. Others have used it to argue against these things and claim that they are the opposite of what the Bible teaches. One reason for these disagreements is that people interpret the Bible in different ways.

Some Christians interpret the Bible literally. They believe that God dictated the words to the authors, who recorded them with perfect accuracy. These Christians claim that the Bible is **infallible** and contains *literal* truth. This means that every part of the Bible is historically and scientifically accurate, so if scientists or historians say something that contradicts the Bible then they must be wrong. For example, in the first book of the Bible, Genesis, it says that God created everything in six days. These Christians therefore believe that scientists are wrong when they say that life evolved over millions of years.

Charles Darwin published his theory of evolution in 1859 and it is now widely accepted. However, Christians who interpret the Bible literally reject this theory.

Liberal Christians believe that although God inspired and directed the authors of the Bible, he left them free to express themselves in their own way. Because of this, liberal Christians accept that the Bible may contain some human errors. They emphasise that the Bible was written by ancient people living in very different societies from Christians today. Therefore, it is acceptable to interpret the Bible in a way that is appropriate for the modern world. For example, attitudes to women in modern Britain are very different from attitudes in biblical times. Therefore, parts of the Bible that might be seen as sexist today should be interpreted in a way that fits with modern views on gender.

Liberal Christians also think that many parts of the Bible are myths or metaphors. These parts of the Bible contain *spiritual truths* about God and humans, but they are not factually accurate. For example, they do not consider the creation story in Genesis 1 as a scientific description of how God made everything in six days. They interpret it as a myth, showing that God is the powerful creator of everything.

Activity

In a table, make a list of reasons why basing one's life on the teachings of a book might be seen as both a good and a bad thing.

Key vocabulary

authoritative Viewed as having power and being worthy of trust and respect

Gospels The first four books of the New Testament, about the life and teachings of Jesus, possibly named after their authors Matthew, Mark, Luke and John

infallible Containing no faults or errors

liberal Open to new ideas and less concerned with tradition

New Testament The last 27 books of the Bible, written shortly after Jesus's lifetime

Old Testament The first 39 books of the Bible, written before the birth of Jesus

Check your understanding

1 Where does the word 'Bible' come from?

2 When and by whom was the Bible written?

3 Why was it important for Christians to agree on the contents of the Bible?

4 Create a table showing the differences between literal and liberal views of the Bible.

5 'The Bible is infallible.' Discuss this statement.

Unit 2: Christianity in the modern world

Is Britain a Christian country?

Christianity has been an important part of British life for over 1400 years, but in recent decades beliefs have changed, raising the question of whether it is right to call Britain a Christian country.

How did Christianity reach Britain?

In the early days of Christianity, Britain was the westernmost point of the Roman Empire. It was a long way for missionaries to travel, and most people in Britain worshipped many gods and goddesses. In CE 597, however, a team of 40 missionaries sent by Pope Gregory and led by a monk named Augustine arrived in Britain. Their aim was to spread the Christian message.

On their journey, the missionaries heard stories about how fierce the British people were. They grew frightened and wanted to turn back, but Pope Gregory encouraged the missionaries to keep going. When they arrived in England, they were warmly welcomed, and were surprised to find that there were already many Christians living there. Within a year of their arrival, around 10,000 people had been baptised, including the King of Kent, Ethelbert. Ethelbert gave Augustine a gift of land in Canterbury, and this became the site of the country's first cathedral. It was not long before most people in Britain were Christians.

Pope Gregory blessing Augustine before his mission to Britain.

Christianity's impact and influence

Christianity is still an influential part of British life. This can be seen in the number of churches across the country and in the education system, where 30 per cent of children attend a Christian faith school. When someone becomes king or queen, he or she also becomes head of the Church of England, and is given the title 'Defender of the Faith'. The national anthem refers to God three times and two of the main holiday periods in Britain – Christmas and Easter – are Christian festivals.

The Archbishop of Canterbury

The king or queen is automatically the head of the Church of England, but the Archbishop of Canterbury is the Church's religious leader. The Church provides the Prime Minister with a shortlist of two names and, on the monarch's behalf, the Prime Minister chooses one of them to be Archbishop of Canterbury. The Archbishop lives at Lambeth Palace in London. The 105th Archbishop of Canterbury, Justin Welby, was appointed in 2012.

The letters 'FD' around the Queen's head on a one pound coin stand for *Fidei Defensor*, which means 'Defender of the Faith' in Latin.

Belief in Britain today

Today, more people in Britain follow Christianity than any other religion, but in recent years Britain has become more **secular** and more religiously diverse. We know about religious belief from national censuses – government surveys taken every 10 years to find out about the people living in Britain. Between 2001 and 2011, the percentage of people describing themselves as Christian decreased from 72 per cent to 59 per cent. The percentage of people following no religion increased from 15 per cent to 25 per cent. In 2011, 10 per cent of the population followed religions other than Christianity.

Christian responses to change

In the past, Sunday was a day for resting and going to church. Shops and businesses were closed. There are still laws limiting shop opening hours on Sundays, but declining church attendance is a challenge for Christians in Britain. They have responded to this in different ways.

Some liberal Christians argue that people are put off going to church because Christianity seems old-fashioned and has too many rules. They think that Christianity needs to adapt in order to thrive in modern Britain. Others say that Christian beliefs and teachings should not be changed. Instead, churches should change the style of their services to attract more people. For example, some churches have informal services with modern music. Some also meet in converted warehouses, coffee shops or theatres rather than in church buildings.

Fact

According to the 1841 census, around 40 per cent of people attended church regularly. Today, this is approximately 5 per cent, and fewer people baptise their children or get married in church than in the past.

Alpha

Many Christians believe that they should try to convert others to Christianity through evangelism – spreading the message of Jesus. One way in which churches evangelise is through Alpha. This is a 10-week course attended by non-Christians who want to find out more about the religion. Each week, people on the course have a meal together, listen to a talk about Christianity and take part in a group discussion about what they have heard.

Activity

Draw a table with two columns, one headed 'Britain is a Christian country' and the other headed 'Britain is not a Christian country'. In bullet points, give as many reasons as you can for both sides.

Key vocabulary

secular Non-religious

Check your understanding

1. Why were missionaries surprised when they arrived in Britain? What happened then?
2. In what ways could you say that Christianity is influential in Britain today?
3. What do the censuses show about belief in Britain?
4. Explain how different Christians might respond to declining church attendance.
5. 'Britain is a Christian country.' Discuss this statement.

Prayer and publicity

In 2015, an advert by the Church of England was banned from cinemas causing a great deal of controversy. Was it right for the advert to be banned?

In December 2015, the Church of England made a 60-second advert to promote its new website. It was intended to be shown in cinemas before the new *Star Wars* film, due to be released just before Christmas. The advert showed different people saying a line from a prayer found in the Bible called the Lord's Prayer. Jesus taught this prayer to his disciples, and Christians around the world have recited it for 2000 years. In the advert, the people praying included weightlifters at a gym, a sheep farmer, a gospel choir, the Archbishop of Canterbury, refugees and a grieving son. After the prayer, the advert claimed that 'prayer is for everyone', and showed the address for the new website.

The Digital Cinema Media (DCM) agency refused to show the advert in its cinemas, which include Odeon, Cineworld and Vue. The agency claimed that it might offend those of 'differing faiths and no faiths' and stated that its policy was 'not to run advertising connected to personal beliefs, specifically those related to politics or religion'. A spokesperson explained: 'Our cinemas have found that showing such advertisements carries the risk of upsetting or offending audiences.'

Justin Welby, the Archbishop of Canterbury, took part in the Church of England advert that was banned from cinemas.

Limiting free speech?

This decision caused passionate responses from different people. The Archbishop of Canterbury suggested that DCM should 'let the public judge for themselves rather than be censored or dictated to'.

Richard Dawkins who is an **atheist** agreed, saying: 'I strongly object to suppressing the ads on the grounds that they might "offend" people. If anybody is "offended" by something so trivial as a prayer, they deserve to be offended.' However, Dawkins also thought that DCM was making a business decision based on what it thought its customers wanted rather than deliberately limiting freedom of speech.

The Equality and Human Rights Commission, however, *was* concerned that the ban limited free speech. It said: 'There is no right not to be offended in the UK; what is offensive is very subjective and lies in the eye of the beholder. This does not mean groups or individuals are free to express themselves without restriction. Freedom of expression can be and is restricted but only in order to prevent violence, abuse or discrimination for example. There is nothing in law that prevents Christian organisations promoting their faith through adverts.'

> ❝ Our Father in heaven,
> hallowed be your name,
> your kingdom come,
> your will be done,
> on earth as in heaven.
> Give us today our daily
> bread.
> And forgive us our sins
> as we forgive those who
> sin against us.
> Lead us not into temptation
> but deliver us from evil.
> For the kingdom, the power
> and the glory are yours
> now and for ever.
> Amen. ❞
>
> The Lord's Prayer

Fact

Although the advert was not shown in cinemas, it received much publicity. Within three days of appearing on YouTube, it had been viewed more than 300,000 times.

❝ I'm sorry, but the whole thing stinks. If you are offended by the Lord's Prayer you are too easily offended. It's a 60-second ad, for goodness' sake. Just munch on your popcorn and ignore it. For others, it might just offer a welcome reminder that, when it comes to places of worship, there are – even at this time of year – still alternatives to the great cathedrals of Westfield shopping centre. ❞

Giles Fraser, Church of England priest and journalist

❝ The Church of England is arrogant to imagine it has an automatic right to foist its opinions upon a captive audience who have paid good money for a completely different experience. The Church does not hesitate to ban things that it deems inappropriate from its own church halls – things like yoga. The cinema chains are simply exercising the same right. ❞

Terry Sanderson, president of the National Secular Society

❝ People pay money to go to the cinema, very diverse audiences, and they really don't want religion dictating to them. [...] The C of E [Church of England] is perfectly entitled to make its views known, but it should do so from the pulpit. But of course they can't get many people to go to church so they want to take their message to the cinemas [ ] In the end they've got even more publicity through this ban. ❞

John Hegarty, a leading figure in advertising

Activity

Write a letter to either DCM or the Church of England explaining your view on whether the Lord's Prayer advert should have been shown in cinemas.

Key vocabulary

atheist Someone who does not believe in God or gods

In 2009, a group of atheists advertised their beliefs on London buses. Several Christian groups responded with their own adverts.

Check your understanding

1. What is the Lord's Prayer?
2. What happened in the Church of England advert?
3. Why did DCM refuse to allow the advert to be shown in its cinemas?
4. Explain two different atheist responses to the ban.
5. 'The Church of England's advert should have been banned from cinemas.' Discuss this statement.

Unit 2: Christianity in the modern world
Should women lead the Church?

As Western attitudes change, Christians have debated whether women should lead the Church. Why has this caused so much disagreement?

Changing attitudes

In the past, it was normal in Britain for men to work and provide income for their family while women looked after the children and the home. Over the last 60 years, people's attitudes to gender have changed significantly, and most people now believe that men and women should have equal opportunities to do the same jobs. In 1975, a law was passed called the Sex Discrimination Act. This law made it illegal for employers to choose someone for a job based on gender. The law does not apply to appointing church leaders, but as attitudes in society have changed the question of whether women should lead churches has caused much debate and division among Christians.

Although it is possible for women to be Anglican priests and bishops, there are still members of the Church of England who do not think this should be allowed.

In the Catholic Church, women have never been allowed to become priests, bishops, cardinals or the Pope. However, many Christians argue that the Bible was written in a **patriarchal** culture and that first-century views should not be continued in a modern world where gender equality is highly valued. In the Church of England, the first female priest was **ordained** in 1994, and the first female bishop was ordained in 2014.

Adam and Eve

In Genesis, God creates the first man, Adam. He then creates the first woman, Eve, saying: 'It is not good for the man to be alone. I will make a helper suitable for him' (Genesis 2.18). Some people argue that this Bible verse suggests women are inferior to men, because it describes them as men's 'helpers', created to stop men from being lonely. Furthermore, when God created Adam and Eve, he warned them not to eat the fruit from one particular tree, but Eve disobeys God by doing so. Eve was the first to sin and then she tempted Adam to do the same. Some Christians have interpreted this as showing that women are the weaker sex.

The Fall of Man by Albrecht Dürer, showing Eve tempting Adam with the apple.

The missionary Paul wrote many letters to Christians he met on his travels. Thirteen of these letters are included in the Bible. In them, Paul gives his views on women:

66 Women should remain silent in the churches. They are not allowed to speak, but must be in submission, as the Law says. If they want to enquire about something, they should ask their own husbands at home; for it is disgraceful for a woman to speak in the church. 99

1 Corinthians 14.34–35

Many Christians believe that Paul was against women leading the Church. However, in the same letter he also wrote:

66 Woman is not independent of man, nor is man independent of woman. For as woman was made from man, in the same way man is born of woman; and it is God who brings everything into existence. 99

1 Corinthians 11.11–12

In another letter written to the Galatians, Paul also suggests that all Christians are equal:

66 There is neither Jew nor gentile, slave nor free, male nor female, for you are all one in Christ Jesus. 99

Galatians 3.28

Women in the New Testament

There is no record in the New Testament of Jesus's views on the roles of men and women, but his attitude towards women was radical for a Jewish man living in the Middle East 2000 years ago. At this time, it was unheard of for a man to discuss religious ideas with a woman. Often men would not even talk to their own wife when they were in public. Jesus surprised his disciples by openly spending time talking with women, even those who were known to have lived sinful lives.

The first people that Jesus appeared to after his resurrection were women. Jesus told them to spread the message that he was alive. Some Christians think this shows that Jesus viewed women as reliable and trustworthy. If he did not think this, then he would not have trusted them to share the message that would become the basis of Christianity.

For centuries, artists have depicted the scene from the Bible of Jesus appearing to Mary Magdalene after his resurrection.

Key vocabulary

ordained Made a priest or bishop in a special ceremony

patriarchal A way of describing a culture that is dominated and controlled by men

Check your understanding

1 How do attitudes to female leadership differ between denominations?

2 Why might someone say that Genesis suggests women are weaker than men?

3 Explain how two contrasting quotes about women from Paul could be interpreted.

4 Why was Jesus's attitude to women surprising?

5 'Men and women are not viewed as equal in Christianity.' Discuss this statement.

Slavery and the Crusades

Why might people be critical of the way some Christians behaved in the past?

Christianity is not just about believing certain things. It is also about trying to live in a way that pleases God. Protestants believe that the Bible tells them how they should live. For Catholics, the teachings of the Church and the Pope are also important.

What does the Bible say?

Genesis says that God created humans in his own 'image' and 'likeness'. This teaches Christians about the **sanctity of life**. The Bible also says that while Jesus was on earth, he helped people in need and taught his followers the Golden Rule: 'Do for others what you want them to do for you: this is the meaning of the Law of Moses and of the teachings of the prophets' (Matthew 7.12).

These biblical teachings affect the way that Christians live. For example, they might choose to support Christian charities like Christian Aid, which aim to eradicate world poverty and create a fairer world. However, there have also been times when Christians have not behaved well towards others.

Slavery

Between the seventeenth and nineteenth centuries, white Europeans and Americans captured black Africans and transported them to the USA in terrible conditions. Many Africans died on the slave ships. Those that survived were sold to wealthy white Christians and forced to work for them. Some slave-owners tried to justify slavery by saying that in Paul's letters in the Bible he refers to slaves and masters, showing he accepted slavery. However, other Christians thought that keeping people as slaves was against the Bible's teachings about equality and the sanctity of life. Christians led campaigns to abolish slavery in many countries, including the USA and Britain.

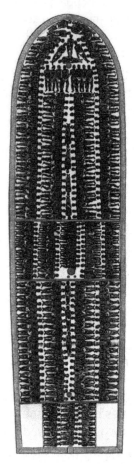

Africans were packed like cargo into the slave ships and transported to the USA.

After slavery was abolished, racism remained a problem. Christian leaders such as Martin Luther King used Bible teachings to argue that racism is wrong. King encouraged his supporters to peacefully protest against racism and to follow Jesus's teachings to love and pray for their enemies.

Martin Luther King stressed that God created all humans equally in God's image.

War and pacifism

The Christian belief in the sanctity of life affects attitudes to violence and war. Some Christians, including Quakers, are pacifists. This means they believe that all disputes should be solved peacefully. Quakers refuse to fight in wars. During the World War I, some people mocked them for not fighting by giving them white feathers – a symbol of cowardice (being afraid). Other Christians believe that although one of the **Ten Commandments** in the Bible is 'Do not murder', there are extreme circumstances where violence might be necessary to prevent a greater evil from happening.

The Crusades

Although most Christians today believe that violence should be a last resort, this has not always been the case. In the eleventh to thirteenth centuries, Christians fought in wars known as the Crusades. In 1079, a powerful group of Muslims conquered Jerusalem. Christians were concerned that these Muslim rulers might ban them from visiting the Church of the Holy Sepulchre in Jerusalem. This was a popular **pilgrimage** site for Christians because they believed it was where Jesus was resurrected. Christians were also worried that Islam was expanding into the 'Christian' city of Constantinople (present-day Istanbul).

In 1095, Pope Urban II called for an army of 'soldiers of Christ' to march across Europe as part of what became known the First Crusade. Its aim was to defend Constantinople and conquer Jerusalem. The Pope promised that those taking part would be forgiven for their past sins and guaranteed a place in heaven.

Approximately 60,000 Crusaders began the journey of nearly 5000 kilometres. To avoid starvation, some of them ate dogs and rats. There were even rumours that they ate human flesh. The crusaders looted many villages and killed a large number of Jews on the journey. Only 15,000 Crusaders survived the 4-year journey to Jerusalem. Despite their decreased

Peter the Hermit encouraging people to join the First Crusade.

number, they managed to conquer the city. Once inside, the Crusaders looted the Islamic holy site known as the Dome of the Rock and massacred the Muslim and Jewish population. Many were tortured and burned alive.

> ### Fact
>
> Influential preachers such as Peter the Hermit helped recruit fighters. Many peasants believed that Peter had received a letter from God, promising that the Holy Spirit would protect the Crusaders, and that their victory would bring paradise on earth.

> ### Key vocabulary
>
> **pilgrimage** A journey taken to a place of religious importance
>
> **sanctity of life** The belief that all life is God-given and sacred
>
> **Ten Commandments** Laws for how people should live, given to Moses by God in the Old Testament

Check your understanding

1. Where do different Christians find guidance on moral issues?
2. What is meant by the 'sanctity of life' and the 'Golden Rule'?
3. How were Christians involved in maintaining and abolishing slavery?
4. Describe the events of the First Crusade.
5. 'Christians always value human life.' Discuss this statement.

Unit 2: Christianity in the modern world
What is the 'problem of evil'?

Christians believe that God is all good (omnibenevolent), all powerful (omnipotent) and all knowing (omniscient), so why does he allow evil and suffering in the world?

Evil and suffering

The 'problem of evil' is an argument or theory that has been around since the time of the ancient Greeks. There are four main stages to the argument:

- If God is omnibenevolent, he would have the desire to get rid of evil and suffering, because it causes so much unhappiness.

- If God is omnipotent, he would have the ability to get rid of evil, because he can do anything.

- If God is omniscient, he would know how to get rid of evil, because he knows everything.

- There is evil in the world, so either God does not exist or he is not omnibenevolent, omnipotent and omniscient.

The 'free will' defence

Throughout history, Christians have tried to show that God can be omnibenevolent, omnipotent and omniscient, even though there is evil and suffering in the world. One argument is that because God is omnibenevolent he did not want to create humans who would be like puppets, so he gave them the good gift of **free will** to choose their own paths through life. Sometimes humans choose the path of evil, which causes suffering. The only way that God could get rid of evil and suffering would be to get rid of free will.

Some people criticise the free will defence because it only explains evil and suffering caused by humans, not that caused by natural events such as earthquakes, hurricanes and disease. They also argue that if God knows people will choose evil, then free will is not a loving gift for God to give.

The devil

Some Christians believe that evil and suffering are caused by the devil. The devil is not mentioned many times in the Bible, but there is a story in the **Apocrypha** that says that he was originally an angel who was expelled from heaven for refusing to worship God. Some Christians explain natural disasters as the work of the devil and other evil spiritual beings.

Some editions of the Bible include the Apocrypha between the Old and New Testaments.

A test of faith

Some Christians say that suffering is God's way of testing and strengthening people's faith. Through suffering, people can also develop positive virtues such as patience, courage, empathy and love. Others disagree with this, arguing that suffering often has the opposite effect on people, or that the good achieved often does not outweigh the pain experienced. Furthermore, Christians might say that if God is omnibenevolent and omnipotent, he would find a more loving way to develop people's faith and virtues than making them suffer.

Punishment

In the past, many Christians viewed suffering as a punishment from God. During the fourteenth century, the Black Death killed approximately half of the population of Europe. At the time, many people thought that God had sent this plague to punish people for their sins.

A minority of Christians still believe that God chooses to punish people for sinning by sending natural disasters. However, most Christians do not believe that an omnibenevolent God would want to punish people so severely.

> ### Fact
>
> In the Bible, Jesus describes the devil as 'the father of lies'. He also says 'I saw Satan fall like lightning from heaven', which could be seen as a reference to the story about him in the Apocrypha.

Flagellants

During the Black Death, people known as flagellants travelled around the country carrying crosses and publicly whipping themselves to seek forgiveness for their sins so that God would not punish them. Although the Pope condemned what they were doing, flagellants would whip themselves until they were bruised, swollen and bleeding.

Mystery

Many Christians believe that both life and God's purposes are mysteries that cannot be fully understood by humans. They argue that we should accept that we do not know why suffering occurs, but should trust that God knows best for us.

> ### Key vocabulary
>
> **Apocrypha** A collection of books that were not included in the Bible
>
> **free will** The ability to choose between right and wrong

> ### Check your understanding
>
> ❶ What is the 'problem of evil'?
> ❷ Explain the 'free will' defence.
> ❸ Why might someone disagree that suffering is a test of faith?
> ❹ How else might a Christian explain why God allows evil and suffering?
> ❺ 'The existence of evil proves that the Christian God does not exist.' Discuss this statement.

What is Charismatic Christianity?

Charismatic Christians emphasise having a close, personal relationship with God and experiencing the Holy Spirit. How does this influence their church services?

Christians worship God in many different ways. Some church services are quiet, formal events where people perform rituals and recite prayers and creeds. In Charismatic churches, however, services are less formal and people participating are said to be led by the Holy Spirit. Charismatic churches are not all the same, but they have some common features.

Worship

In a Charismatic church, a leader plans the service, but this plan might change if the leader thinks that the Holy Spirit is taking the service in a different direction. Services usually begin with a period of worshipping God through song. Musicians often play modern songs of worship, accompanied by guitars, drums and keyboard. The words of the songs are displayed on a big screen so that the **congregation** can sing along.

People can feel quite emotional during this time of worship and they may be very expressive in their body movements. For example, worshippers might clap their hands or wave them in the air, or even dance. They may also cry or laugh, which they describe as being 'drunk with the Holy Spirit'.

The Yoido Full Gospel Church is a Charismatic church in South Korea, which can hold 26,000 people. Most Sundays, over 250,000 people attend services there, making it the best attended church in the world.

Testimony

During a Charismatic service, people may share a message, or testimony, with the rest of the congregation. They might talk about how they were converted to Christianity, about a prayer that has been answered or about a miracle they have seen.

Spiritual gifts

Charismatic Christians believe that the Holy Spirit gives individuals different **spiritual gifts**. The purpose of these gifts is to strengthen the faith of the Church. These might be:

- Prophecy – This can include having knowledge of a situation that a person is facing, or passing on God's message to someone, perhaps to provide comfort or admonishment.

Fact

Some Christians think that Charismatic Christianity is too focused on spiritual experiences and has lost sight of what the religion is really about, such as the teachings of the Bible.

- Speaking in tongues – Charismatic Christians believe that God gives some people the ability to speak to him in a special spiritual language. This language only makes sense to those who have the gift of interpreting tongues.

- Healing – Many Charismatic Christians believe that God performs miracles such as healing people. He also gives some people the power to perform healings. Charismatic Christians have healing services in which they pray for people who are unwell. Sometimes people will start shaking or fall over backwards whilst being prayed for and this is often explained as a powerful experience of the Holy Spirit.

Charismatic worship is often very expressive and can be an emotional experience for believers.

Persecution of Nigerian Christians

Charismatic Christianity is popular in Africa. In Nigeria, around half the population are Christians, and many are Charismatic Christians. Nigerian Christians often face persecution. In December 2011, a militant Islamic group called Boko Haram told Christians in northern parts of Nigeria that they had three days to leave the area. This was followed by two days of church bombings in which 26 Christians died and 8 more were shot. Some Nigerian churches have banned women from carrying handbags to church because they are afraid that a terrorist might bring in a bomb. Other churches have installed metal detectors to make sure no one can bring in a gun.

The site of a church bombing in Nigeria carried out by Boko Haram.

66 Many Nigerians have been killed, wounded or mutilated, kidnapped and deprived of everything: their loved ones, their land, their means of subsistence, their dignity and their rights. Many have not been able to return to their homes. Believers, both Christian and Muslim, have experienced a common tragic outcome, at the hands of people who claim to be religious, but who instead abuse religion. 99

Pope Francis in a letter to Nigerian bishops in 2015

Key vocabulary

congregation people who attend a religious service

spiritual gifts Supernatural abilities given by God, for example, the ability to prophesy or speak in tongues

Activity

Imagine you have visited a Charismatic Church. Write a diary entry explaining what you saw and how a Charismatic Christian would explain it.

Check your understanding

1 How is a Charismatic church service different from some other church services?
2 What might happen during Charismatic worship?
3 Explain two of the spiritual gifts in Charismatic Christianity.
4 Why might someone be critical of Charismatic Christianity?
5 Explain how Christians have been persecuted in Nigeria and how some churches have responded.

Unit 2: Christianity in the modern world
The persecution of Christians

Between 2006 and 2010, Christians were persecuted in 139 different countries, but who is persecuting them, and why?

Christians are persecuted by a variety of different groups and for many reasons. It can be difficult to find out precise facts about Christian persecution because it is often carried out secretly. Experts think that as many as 8000 Christians are martyred every year, but it might be far more. Below are four examples of Christian persecution.

North Korea

North Korea is thought to be the most dangerous place in the world to be a Christian. Hundreds of thousands of Christians there have disappeared, but there may be 200,000–400,000 still living in the country. Around 25 per cent of these Christians are held in prison camps, where they are tortured and made to do difficult work in terrible conditions. There have also been reports of Christians being publicly executed.

North Koreans must worship Kim Jong-un.

Christians are persecuted because they refuse to worship the country's leader, Kim Jong-un. The North Korean authorities try to keep their persecution of Christians secret from those outside the country. When world leaders and other important people visit North Korea, the government has been known to fill churches with actors to make it look as though religious freedom is allowed.

> 66 The persecution of Christians throughout much of the Middle East, sub-Saharan Africa, Asia and elsewhere is one of the crimes against humanity of our time, and I am appalled at the lack of protest it has evoked. That people in the twenty-first century are being murdered, terrorised, victimised, intimidated and robbed of their liberties because of the way they worship God is a moral outrage, a political scandal and a desecration of faith itself. I believe that God himself weeps at the evils being committed in His name. 99
> Former Chief Rabbi Lord Sacks

Orissa, India

Orissa is a state in north-east India where there is a small minority of Christians. In 2008, a Hindu man was killed there. This sparked riots in which Hindu radicals killed 500 Christians with machetes. Thousands of other Christians were injured and more than 200 churches were burned or torn down. Five thousand homes were destroyed, and many people deserted their villages and fled to the jungles. They were warned that if they refused to convert to Hinduism they would be killed if they returned.

The remains of a Christian home burned down in Orissa, India, in 2008.

Myanmar

In 2007, a report appeared in Myanmar called 'Programme to destroy the Christian religion in Burma'. (Burma is another name for Myanmar.) It is thought that the report came from the Myanmar government. The first line of the report stated: 'There shall be no home where the Christian religion is practised.' It then gave guidance on what must be done to get rid of Christianity, saying: 'The Christian religion is very gentle – identify and utilise its weakness.' The guidance said that anyone who spread the Christian message should be put in prison.

In recent years, there have also been reports of churches being burned down in Myanmar. Christians are persecuted because the leaders want all people in Myanmar to follow the official religion, Buddhism. Many Christians have been driven out of their homes. In October 2010, the Myanmar Air Force launched helicopter attacks on areas where Christians lived, killing thousands.

Baghdad, Iraq

Christianity has probably existed in Iraq since the first century. Today, Christians in Iraq live in constant fear of violence. There are 65 churches in the capital city of Baghdad. Since 2003, 40 of these have been bombed at least once. In 2010, a group of Islamic **militants** entered a Catholic cathedral during the service. They killed 58 people, including the priests leading the service. On Christmas Day 2013, two bombs exploded in areas of Baghdad where Christians live. One was set off next to a Catholic church in which Christians were worshipping, killing 24 people. A second bomb exploded near a market, killing 11 more.

Despite persecution, Christians in Iraq continue to practise their religion.

In 1991, there were approximately 1.5 million Christians living in Iraq. No one knows how many remain today. Some experts think it may be 500,000, but others believe it could be as low as 150,000. Some of them have fled the country, but many others have been killed.

Activity

Create a leaflet raising awareness of the persecution of Christians in the world today. You should include at least three case studies, giving examples of how and why Christians are persecuted.

Key vocabulary

militants Individuals or groups who use violence to spread their ideas

---

Check your understanding

1 In how many countries were Christians persecuted between 2006 and 2010?
2 Approximately how many Christians are martyred each year?
3 Why and how are Christians persecuted in North Korea?
4 What was the report in Myanmar called and what did it say?
5 How are Christians being persecuted by Islamic militants?

Unit 2: Christianity in the modern world
Knowledge organiser

Key vocabulary

Apocrypha A collection of books that were not included in the Bible

atheist Someone who does not believe in God or gods

authoritative Viewed as having power and being worthy of trust and respect

congregation people who attend a religious service

free will The ability to choose between right and wrong

Gospels The first four books of the New Testament, about the life and teachings of Jesus, possibly named after their authors Matthew, Mark, Luke and John

infallible Containing no faults or errors

liberal Open to new ideas and less concerned with tradition

militants Individuals or groups who use violence to spread their ideas

New Testament The last 27 books of the Bible, written shortly after Jesus's lifetime.

Old Testament The first 39 books of the Bible, written before the birth of Jesus

ordained Made a priest or bishop in a special ceremony

patriarchal A way of describing a culture that is dominated and controlled by men

pilgrimage A journey taken to a place of religious importance

sanctity of life The belief that all life is God-given and sacred

secular Non-religious

spiritual gifts Supernatural abilities given by God, for example, the ability to prophesy or speak in tongues

Ten Commandments Laws for how people should live, given to Moses by God in the Old Testament

Key facts

- The Christian holy book is the Bible, which is divided into the Old and New Testaments. These were written by many people over centuries. Christians of different denominations interpret the Bible in different ways.

- Britain has been a Christian country for around 1400 years, since missionaries travelled to convert people in the sixth century. The leader of the Church of England is the Archbishop of Canterbury.

- Some Christians attend Charismatic Churches, where there is a belief in spiritual gifts such as speaking in tongues and the ability to prophesy.

- Although Christians today believe in the sanctity of life, some Christians in the past took part in the Crusades and the slave trade.

- In the modern world, Christianity faces many challenges, including declining numbers and criticism of its influence, as seen by the controversy surrounding the Church of England advert being shown in cinemas in 2015. Censuses show that Britain is becoming more secular and more religiously diverse.

- Because Christians disagree about how to interpret the Bible, literal and liberal interpretations can lead to different views among Christians about many issues, including how the universe was created and whether women should lead the Church.

- The 'problem of evil' remains a challenge to the Christian idea of God.

- Between 2006 and 2010, Christians were persecuted in over two-thirds of the countries in the world including Iraq, India, North Korea, Nigeria and Myanmar.

A youth choir sings and dances at a church in Morogoro, Tanzania, East Africa.

Key people

Archbishop of Canterbury The leader of the Church of England

Augustine Monk who led a team of Christian missionaries to Britain

Martin Luther King An American civil rights leader and Christian who argued that racism was wrong

Pope Gregory The Pope who sent Augustine and missionaries to Britain in CE 597

Pope Urban II The Pope who launched the first crusade in 1095

Justin Welby The current Archbishop of Canterbury

Westminster Abbey in London is one of the most famous churches in Britain. The current building has stood for approximately 700 years.

Islam

History and belief

In this first section of this book, you will examine the dramatic events that led to the beginnings of Islam and will discover how it spread through Arabia and beyond at an astonishing speed. You will also find out how a disagreement about who should lead the religion after the death of its founder caused it to split into two groups, which still exist today. You will also explore some of the beliefs of Muslims, for example, what God is like, who he has sent to earth as prophets and what happens when we die.

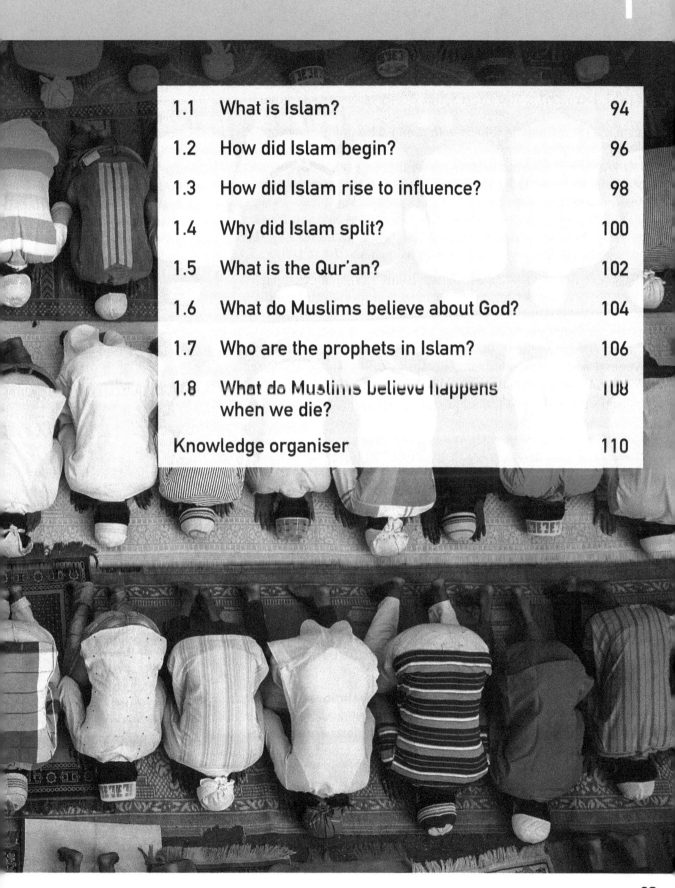

What is Islam?

Islam is the second-largest and fastest-growing religion in the world. How did it start and what do its followers believe?

Islam is a **monotheistic** religion with over 1.6 billion followers around the world, who are known as Muslims. In 1900, 12 per cent of people on earth followed Islam, but experts predict that 30 per cent of the global population will be Muslims by 2050. This means that that there will be nearly as many Muslims as Christians (31 per cent) by 2050. One key reason for the growth of Islam is the high birth rate amongst Muslims. Between 2010 and 2015, Muslim women had, on average, 3.1 babies, compared with 2.7 babies for Christian women and 2.4 for Hindus.

The Arabic word '*islam*' literally means 'submission'. Submission is when you willingly accept, surrender to or give yourself to something or someone you believe to be greater than you. This is a helpful way of understanding Islam: Muslims believe that there is one God who created the world out of nothing, and that he has complete control over their lives and what happens to them after they die. The Arabic word '*muslim*' means 'one who submits to God'. Muslims believe that they should live their whole lives for God.

The beginnings of Islam

The story of Islam begins in Arabia approximately 1400 years ago, in 570 CE. This is the year in which **Muhammad**, whom Muslims believe to be the last of all the **prophets**, was born. Sometimes you will see the letters 'PBUH' after Muhammad's name. These letters stand for 'peace be upon him' and they show respect. Muslims may also say 'peace be upon him' after saying Muhammad's name.

Islam was founded after the other Abrahamic religions (Judaism and Christianity), but Muslims often refer to Jews and Christians as 'People of the Book'. This is because Muslims believe that God – '**Allah**' in Arabic – revealed himself to the earlier prophets mentioned in the Bible, such as Abraham, Moses and Jesus. However, Muslims believe that over time the message of these prophets was changed and corrupted, and so God sent one final prophet – Muhammad.

Muslims believe that God revealed messages (**revelations**) to Muhammad about what people should believe and how they should live their lives. They consider these revelations to be perfect and final. The revelations that were given to Muhammad were memorised by his followers and collected in a book called the **Qur'an** after his death. The Qur'an is written in Arabic, but there are translations in English and other languages.

> **Fact**
>
> Followers of Islam are called Muslims, but when someone is describing something that is typical of Islam he or she will use the word 'Islamic' – for example, Islamic music, writing or architecture.

The Sultan Ahmed Mosque in Istanbul, Turkey, is also known as the Blue Mosque because of all its blue tiles.

> **Fact**
>
> Muslims meet together to pray in buildings known as **mosques** (*masjid* in Arabic, which means a 'place of prostration' – bowing down). People can pray in mosques at any time, but noon on Friday is when most Muslims attend.

Did Muhammad really live?

Most historians agree that Muhammad was a real person. However, when considering events from hundreds or thousands of years ago, it can be difficult to separate fact and legend. Sometimes writers want to influence the way people are remembered, so they may change or exaggerate events. This applies to all of history, not just Islamic history.

Where do Muslims live?

The map below shows which countries have the highest populations of Muslims. Muslims live all over the world, but you can see that Islam is the dominant religion in North Africa and the Middle East. In these regions, most people are Muslim, although they may not all be the same type of Muslim. Just as there are different groups of Jews and Christians, there are also different groups of Muslims, and they have different beliefs and ways of following their religion.

The UK is home to just under 3 million Muslims, meaning Muslims make up approximately 5 per cent of the total UK population. This makes Islam the second-largest religion in the UK, after Christianity.

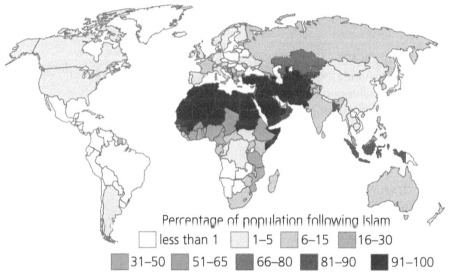

Percentage of population following Islam

less than 1 | 1–5 | 6–15 | 16–30
31–50 | 51–65 | 66–80 | 81–90 | 91–100

A map showing the countries with the highest Muslim populations.

Activity

In pairs, think of stories or events from other religions you have studied where historians might question, or disagree about, whether they really happened.

Key vocabulary

Allah The Arabic word for God

monotheism Belief in one God

mosque The place of worship for Muslims; it literally means 'place of prostration'

Muhammad The final prophet sent by God, to whom God revealed messages (revelations) about what people should believe and how they should live their lives

prophet A messenger of God

Qur'an The holy book of Islam, which Muslims believe contains the word of God; it literally means 'recitation'

revelation A message revealed by God to humans

Check your understanding

1 How has the world population of Muslims changed since 1900?

2 What does the word '*islam*' literally mean and how does this help show what the religion of Islam is about?

3 Who is the last and most important prophet in Islam, and what do Muslims believe about him?

4 Where do Muslims live?

5 'Islam has a lot in common with other religions.' Discuss this statement.

Unit 1: History and belief

How did Islam begin?

How did Muhammad's encounter with the angel Jibril in a cave near Mecca begin a new religion and alter the course of history?

The early life of Muhammad

At the time of Muhammad, there were two main cities in central Arabia – **Medina** and **Mecca** (sometimes spelled 'Madinah' and 'Makkah'). Muhammad was born in Mecca in 570 CE. His father, Abdullah, died before he was born and his mother, Amina, died when he was six, so Muhammad was brought up by his uncle, Abu Talib, who was a trader. Muhammad would accompany his uncle on business trips across the Arabian desert to Syria and gained a reputation as an excellent trader. He was given the nickname al-Amin, which means 'the trustworthy'. At the age of 25, Muhammad married a wealthy businesswoman and widow called Khadija. She was 15 years older than him, but she admired the skills he had learned from his uncle.

Arabia before Islam

Most people in Arabia at this time lived in tribes. Some of these people were followers of Judaism and Christianity, but many tribes were **polytheistic**. The gods they worshipped were often linked to nature and aspects of the environment that played an essential part in people's survival, such as the sun. The Arab tribes believed that these gods would look after and protect them. Muhammad was born into a polytheistic tribe called the Quraysh.

In the seventh century, there was much cruelty, violence and poverty in the city of Mecca. Muhammad disliked this, and he would often retreat to a cool, quiet cave in the mountains outside the city in order to think and pray. It was here in this cave, at the age of 40, that Muhammad had a religious experience that would change his life and the society of Mecca forever. The night on which this happened is called Laylat al-Qadr in Arabic, which can be translated as the Night of Power.

The Arabian Peninsula, where Islam began. A peninsula is land that is surrounded by water on three sides.

The Night of Power

On this night, the angel Jibril (Gabriel) appeared to Muhammad and revealed a message from God. Jibril told Muhammad to recite words that were later recorded in the Qur'an.

Islamic scholars disagree about what exactly happened in the cave. According to one account, Jibril told Muhammad to read from a scroll. When Muhammad said that he could not read, Jibril told him three times '*iqra!*' ('Read!'). On the third time, he placed his hands around Muhammad's waist and squeezed him until the words forced their way

> ### Fact
> The Night of Power is celebrated by Muslims towards the end of the month of **Ramadan**. Muslims will often stay awake praying, as they believe that God is especially forgiving on this night.

into Muhammad's mouth. It was as though the words were being written on his heart and he would never forget them.

Muhammad was still shaking when he returned home to Khadija. She knew her husband was an honest man, so his words must truly be from God. She became the first believer of his message. The second person to become a Muslim was Muhammad's cousin, Ali, followed by one of Muhammad's closest friends, Abu Bakr.

A crowd of people visiting the cave where Muhammad is believed to have received his first revelation from Jibril.

The Qur'an

The Arabic word 'qur'an' means 'recitation' or 'that which is read or recited', because this is how Muhammad received the words. The Night of Power is recorded in **surah** 96 of the Qur'an, which is often known as the 'Blood Clot' chapter, because it says that God created humans from a blood clot. Over the next 23 years, Jibril visited Muhammad with more revelations that were remembered and recorded during his lifetime and collected together after his death, according to Islamic sources.

The Night Journey

According to Islamic tradition, one night in approximately 620 CE Muhammad was in Mecca praying when Jibril suddenly appeared and flew him to Jerusalem on a winged horse. Muhammad prayed and spoke with all the prophets that have ever lived. He then ascended to the heavens and spent time with God, who told him that Muslims should pray five times a day. Muhammad then returned to Jerusalem and flew back to Mecca. Muslims disagree about whether the Night Journey really happened or whether Muhammad saw the events in a vision.

Key vocabulary

Mecca A city in present-day Saudi Arabia; Muhammad was born here in 570 CE

Medina One of the main cities in Arabia in the time of Muhammad (originally called Yathrib)

polytheism Belief in many gods

Ramadan The ninth month of the Islamic year (which is based on the moon)

surah A chapter of the Qur'an; there are 114 surahs in total

Check your understanding

1 When was Muhammad born and when was the Night of Power?

2 Describe Muhammad's early life.

3 What was Arabia like before Islam was established there?

4 In your own words, describe what happened on the Night of Power.

5 What was the Night Journey? Explain different views a Muslim might have about this event.

How did Islam rise to influence?

How did Muhammad combine his radical religious message
with political and military power?

Muhammad the prophet

After the Night of Power, Muhammad began preaching his message in
Mecca. His words were considered radical. Muhammad said that it was
wrong for Meccans to worship many gods. He insisted that there was only
one God, and claimed that this God had given him instructions for how
people should live their lives. In particular, he criticised the worship of **idols**.

This was particularly controversial because Muhammad's own tribe looked
after the idols in Mecca's main holy site, the **Ka'aba**. The leaders of the tribe
did not like Muhammad's radical monotheistic message. They saw it as a threat
to their power and to the income they earned through polytheistic tribes
visiting the Ka'aba on pilgrimage. They tried to persuade him to abandon his
preaching and to join them as the most powerful traders in Mecca. When
Muhammad refused, the leaders of the tribe denied Muhammad's message
and persecuted his followers. They banned Meccans from marrying or trading
with any of Muhammad's followers. Some of them were tortured and killed.

A modern picture of the Ka'aba.

Bilal

One man who was attacked because of his conversion to Islam was a slave
called Bilal. He was one of Muhammad's earliest followers. When Bilal's
master found out that he had converted to Islam he violently tortured
him, but Bilal would not give up his faith. His master was angry that Bilal
regarded God as more important than him and that Bilal would not honour
the many idols that the other Meccans worshipped. His master ordered
that a large stone be placed on Bilal's chest to slowly crush him. Bilal simply
said, 'Ahad, ahad' – 'God is one.' Muhammad was shocked when he heard
about the treatment of Bilal and told his friend Abu Bakr to buy Bilal from
his master. After Bilal was freed from slavery, he became a close friend
of Muhammad.

Bilal became an important
figure in early Islam. Here,
he is calling Muslims to pray
from the top of the Ka'aba.

Muhammad the politician

In 620 CE, while preaching outside Mecca, Muhammad met six men from
the city of Yathrib (Medina). They had heard the message of Islam and
became Muslims. Polytheist, Jewish and Christian tribes all lived in Yathrib,
and they had all been fighting each other for many years. The six men
asked Muhammad to move to Yathrib to help settle the conflicts. Over the
next two years, more people from Yathrib visited Muhammad, pledging
allegiance to him and inviting him to move to their city. In 622 CE, after years

Fact

Yathrib was later named
al-Madinat al-Nabi, 'the
city of the Prophet'. Today
it is known as Medina.

of persecution in Mecca, Muhammad instructed all his followers to travel 320 kilometres (200 miles) north to Yathrib. The emigration of Muhammad and his followers to Medina, as Yathrib became known, is called the **Hijrah**.

One of the first things that Muhammad did when he arrived in Medina was to write the **Constitution of Medina**. This was a set of religious laws that aimed to bring together the Muslim, Jewish, Christian and polytheist tribes who lived there and create a fairer society. It included rules to help widows and orphans and it said that Medina should be a 'sacred place' where no weapons could be carried. This was Muhammad's first attempt at creating a community based on his religious beliefs, and Medina became the first Islamic city-state.

Muhammad the warrior

At the time of Muhammad, there were many violent disputes between tribes across the Arabian Peninsula. In 624 CE, Muslims in Medina were being persecuted by tribes in Mecca. Muhammad led his army of followers into battle to defend the safety of Muslims in Medina against this violence. The Battle of Badr, as this event became known, confirmed that Muhammad was no longer just a prophet and a politician – he was also a strong warrior. As a result of his victory in this battle, more people in Medina accepted Muhammad's authority.

The Battle of Badr occurred in Medina.

After a series of battles between Mecca and Medina, Muhammad finally conquered Mecca in 629 CE. Muhammad had sent a message in advance saying that those who stayed in their homes when his army entered the city would not be harmed. On entering Mecca, Muhammad rode straight for the Ka'aba. He circled it seven times before entering it and destroying all the idols inside of it. He then dedicated the Ka'aba to God.

By the end of Muhammad's life, he was the most influential man in Arabia. He had successfully united the warring tribes of the region under Islamic rule. All of the polytheistic tribes had become Muslims, as well as some of the Jews. Muhammad had combined his radical religious message with political and military power. The world would never be the same again.

> ### Activity
> Make a timeline showing the key dates in the life of Muhammad. Include his birth, marriage, the Night of Power, the Hijrah, the Battle of Badr, conquering Mecca, and Muhammad's death in 632 CE.

Key vocabulary

Constitution of Medina The laws passed by Muhammad in Yathrib when he and his followers first settled there

Hijrah The emigration of Muhammad and his followers to Yathrib (Medina) in 622 CE

idol A picture or object that people worship as part of their religion

Ka'aba A holy site in Mecca which Muhammad dedicated to God after destroying its 360 idols

Check your understanding
1 Why did Muhammad disapprove of idol worship?
2 How did the leaders of Muhammad's tribe react when he told them there was one true God?
3 Describe what happened to Bilal.
4 What was the Constitution of Medina?
5 Was Muhammad a prophet, a politician or a warrior? Explain your answer fully.

Why did Islam split?

How did a disagreement about Muhammad's rightful successor cause Islam to split?

The caliphs

Muhammad died in June 632 CE. His message had spread at a rapid pace, and by the time of his death he had conquered the entire Arabian Peninsula and was widely regarded as a true prophet. In the 30 years after Muhammad's death, the Muslim community was led by four political and religious rulers (**caliphs**), all of whom had been close companions of Muhammad:

1. Abu Bakr (632–634 CE)

2. Umar (634–644 CE)

3. Uthman (644–656 CE)

4. Ali (656–661 CE)

Under these four caliphs, the religion of Islam spread across the world at an astonishing speed. This happened through people converting and invasion.

By 750 CE, the Islamic Empire stretched from the westernmost point of Spain to the eastern edge of India. This empire was known as the **Caliphate** and continued to be ruled over by a succession of caliphs in the centuries that followed.

Abu Bakr

After Muhammad's death, some tribes in the Arabian Peninsula wanted to return to having their own rulers. There were also disagreements between followers of Islam, which threatened to divide the new religious community. The first caliph, Abu Bakr, wanted to make sure that people living in Arabia remained Muslims and lived under Islamic rule. During his reign he often used force to defeat rebellions against him and maintain power.

Abu Bakr, the first caliph was a friend of Muhammad and an early convert to Islam.

> ### Umar's conversion
>
> According to Islamic tradition, the second caliph, Umar, originally despised the new religion of Islam and wanted to murder Muhammad. On his way to carry out this attack, Umar stopped at his sister's house to let her and her husband know what he thought about them becoming Muslims. However, when Umar heard them recite the words of the Qur'an, he converted to Islam on the spot and became a loyal follower of Muhammad. As caliph, he helped Islam expand beyond Arabia, conquering the areas now known as Palestine, Syria, Iraq, Egypt and Iran.

Islam continued to spread fast during Uthman's 12-year rule. Uthman had many supporters, but there were also rebels living in the Caliphate who were opposed to him being leader. This caused violence to break out between different groups of Muslims. In 656 CE, opponents of Uthman broke into his house carrying swords and assassinated him.

The fourth caliph, Ali, was Muhammad's cousin – he was the son of Abu Talib. He was also married to Muhammad's daughter Fatima, making him Muhammad's son-in-law. Ali was elected to lead the community after Uthman had been assassinated, but, despite him being a relative of Muhammad, Ali had many opponents who he had to fight to secure power. One of these was a man called Muawiya, the Muslim governor of Syria, who felt that Ali had not done enough to take revenge on Uthman's killers. Muawiya's opposition to Ali led to a war in which different groups of Muslims fought each other for power. In 661 CE, Ali was assassinated, and Muawiya became the fifth caliph.

Pilgrims and scholars at the shrine of Ali.

Sunni and Shi'a Muslims

After Muhammad's death, there was disagreement amongst Muslims over who should be their leader. Not everyone agreed that Abu Bakr, Umar and Uthman should have been caliphs, and this caused Islam to split into two groups and its followers to become known as **Sunni** Muslims and **Shi'a** Muslims.

The majority of Muslims in the world today (about 85 per cent) are Sunni. They believe that it was correct for Abu Bakr to become leader after Muhammad, because he was Muhammad's closest companion. They also think that Umar, Uthman and Ali were the right people to succeed Abu Bakr. However, there is disagreement amongst Sunni Muslims about whether the caliphs who ruled in the centuries after these four men – who are sometimes known as the four Rightly Guided Caliphs – were rightful rulers.

Shi'a Muslims believe that God told Muhammad that Ali should be his immediate successor and that Muhammad made this clear to his followers in a speech given in the year of his death, 632 CE. They believe that the first three caliphs should not have been the rulers of Muslims. Shi'a Muslims also believe that, after Ali's death, his son Hussein should have succeeded him, not Muawiya, and that leadership of Muslims should have continued to pass down through the descendants of Ali.

Key vocabulary

caliph The Arabic word for the leader of the whole Muslim community after the death of Muhammad; it literally means 'successor'. Sunni Muslims call the first four caliphs 'Rightly Guided Caliphs'

Caliphate The Islamic community ruled over by the caliph

Shi'a A smaller group of Muslims who believe that Ali and his descendants should have succeeded Muhammad as leaders of Islam

Sunni The majority (about 85 per cent) of Muslims across the world who believe that the Rightly Guided Caliphs were rightful successors of Muhammad

Check your understanding

1. What did Abu Bakr do while he was caliph?
2. How did Umar initially feel about Islam and what did he achieve as caliph?
3. Why was there a war between Muslims during Ali's rule?
4. Do Sunni and Shi'a Muslims agree on who should have succeeded Muhammad? Explain your answer.
5. "The caliphs played an important role in the development of Islam." Discuss this statement.

Unit 1: History and belief
What is the Qur'an?

What is in the Qur'an and why is it important to Muslims?

The Qur'an is the most important holy book for Muslims. They believe that it was revealed to Muhammad by God. It is seen as the perfect, literal word of God that gives people guidance on how they should live their lives. The Arabic word *'qur'an'* literally means 'recitation' (saying something aloud). According to tradition, Muhammad could not read, but on the Night of Power the angel Jibril insisted, saying, 'Read!' – *'iqra*!' – three times. Muhammad received a rush of energy and suddenly he was able to repeat the words aloud.

Muslims believe that the beauty and power of the Qur'an can only be fully experienced when it is recited aloud, because this is how it was received by Muhammad. As such, when Muslims read the Qur'an, they do so out loud. Huge respect is given to those who can learn the Qur'an by heart. They are given the special title **hafiz** and will sometimes perform the entire Qur'an to other Muslims. Muslims think that the Qur'an can only be truly read in Arabic, because this was the language spoken by Muhammad when he received it. When the Qur'an is translated, it is no longer the words recited by Muhammad. Translations of the Qur'an, therefore, are seen only as interpretations of or substitutes for the Qur'an, not the holy book itself.

This fragment of the Qur'an, owned by the University of Birmingham, is thought to be one of the oldest in the world. The text is written on sheep – or goatskin and may even have been written by someone who knew Muhammad.

How is the Qur'an arranged?

Muhammad received the Qur'an over a 23-year period of his life. Many Islamic scholars are interested in finding out when Muhammad received particular revelations. In Mecca, Muhammad and his followers were being persecuted, whereas in Medina they had the opportunity to establish their own community, and this is reflected in the revelations received.

Initially, the Qur'an was not written down, but was memorised and passed between people by word of mouth. However, towards the end of his life, Muhammad started to dictate chapters (surahs) to his companions so that they could write them down. These chapters would have originally been written down on pieces of animal bone, leather and palm leaves. Each of the 114 surahs is split into verses. In total, there are over 6000 verses in the Qur'an.

Chapters in the Christian Bible move chronologically through time, like a story. In the Qur'an, however, the surahs are generally arranged in order of length, with the longer surahs at the beginning and the shorter ones at the end. This can be a little confusing – for example, the surah that was revealed first to Muhammad is surah 96.

> **Fact**
>
> After Muhammad's death, the third caliph, Uthman, was worried about the Qur'an changing as new followers recited it in newly conquered regions. He created an official Qur'an and ordered that all other versions should be destroyed. All modern versions of the Qur'an are based on this official Qur'an.

Each surah is named after an object or a subject within it. For example, surah 2 is called 'The Cow', because in it Moses tells people to sacrifice a cow. Surah 29 is called 'The Spider' and surah 35 is called 'The Creator'. The most important surah is the first, 'The Opening', which Muslims must recite five times each day. You can read this surah on page 104.

The perfect word

Some parts of the Qur'an are similar to stories found in Jewish and Christian holy books. However, Muslims believe these contain inaccuracies, so God gave Muhammad his perfect word in order to correct them. Muslims believe that Muhammad is the final prophet, whose message has been recorded with complete accuracy in the Qur'an. There will be no further prophets or revelations from God.

Respecting the Qur'an

In order to show respect to the Qur'an, Muslims will often wash before touching it, and will keep it in a clean place with nothing on top of or above it. The Qur'an should be the only book on the top shelf of a bookcase. It is never placed on the floor and if someone drops or damages it, then he or she might kiss it as a sign of respect. Old, worn-out copies should not be thrown away. Most Muslims agree that old Qur'ans should either be wrapped in cloth and buried deep in the ground or placed in flowing water, weighed down with a heavy stone.

The Qur'an.

Key vocabulary

hafiz Someone who has memorised the Qur'an (a man is a hafiz and a woman is called a hafiza)

Check your understanding

1 What does the Arabic word *'qur'an'* mean?
2 In what language must the Qur'an be recited and why?
3 How was the Qur'an originally passed between people and recorded?
4 Describe two differences between the Qur'an and the Bible.
5 How do Muslims show respect to the Qur'an?

What do Muslims believe about God?

Muslims believe that God is beyond human understanding, so how do they try to describe him?

When Islam began, most people in Mecca were polytheists, worshipping gods linked to nature or the environment. When Muhammad began preaching that there was only one God, it made him unpopular with leaders of his tribe, who were responsible for the Ka'aba and looked after its 360 idols. Muhammad said that there should be no idols and destroyed those in the Ka'aba when he conquered Mecca in 629 CE. Therefore, monotheism – the belief that there is only one God – lies at the very heart of Islam.

What is God like?

Muslims believe that there is nothing greater than God. No words can come close to explaining what God is like – he is beyond anything that humans can think or say. However, Muslims believe that God has revealed some of his characteristics in the Qur'an and other sayings of Muhammad. These characteristics are known as the **99 names of God**. Some of these can be seen in surah 1 below.

Many Muslims memorise the 99 names of God so that they can recite them when they pray. This man is using a subhah – a string of prayer beads – to keep count of the 99 names of God.

The Qur'an teaches that God is the eternal creator of everything. He knows everything, he has power over everything, and he decides when people live and die. The first surah of the Qur'an, 'The Opening', shows God's power by describing him as 'Lord' and 'Master':

> ❝ In the name of God, the Lord of Mercy, the Giver of Mercy! Praise belongs to God, Lord of all worlds, the Lord of Mercy, the Giver of Mercy, Master of the Day of Judgement. It is you we worship; it is you we ask for help. Guide us to the straight path: the path of those You have blessed, those who incur no anger and who have not gone astray. ❞
>
> Qur'an 1:1–7

This first surah also teaches Muslims that God is generous and compassionate. Muslims believe that God is the kindest of all beings, that he loves his creation, and that he will always forgive people for their sins if they are truly sorry. The first surah also teaches that there will be a Day of Judgement, when God will judge all people. Because Muslims believe that God sees everything, they try to live in a way that pleases him.

The first surah of the Qur'an contains seven verses, which emphasise God's greatness and mercy.

Tawhid and shirk

Muslims believe that God is One and there are no Gods other than him. This belief in the oneness of God is called **tawhid**. Anything that goes against tawhid is called **shirk**, which is the Arabic word for the sin of worshipping many gods or idols rather than the one God.

> 66 He is God: there is no god other than Him. It is he who knows what is unseen and what is seen, He is the Lord of Mercy, the Giver of Mercy. He is God: there is no god other than Him, the Controller, the Holy One, Source of Peace, Granter of Security, Guardian over all, the Almighty, the Compeller, the Truly Great; God is far above anything they consider to be His partner. 99
>
> Qur'an 59:22–23

Shirk includes trying to compare something or someone to God or claiming that something is equal to him. For example, if a Muslim said that something was as powerful as God, then this would be shirk. It would also be shirk if a Muslim tried to create a picture or a statue of God. Because God is like nothing on earth, he is beyond human imagination, so making an image of him would be idolatry. The Christian belief in the Trinity would also be seen as shirk, because it states that God exists as Father, Son and Holy Spirit.

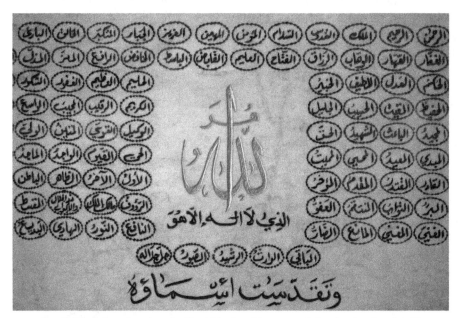

Muslims believe that drawing God is shirk. For this reason, it is common for the 99 names of God found in the Qur'an to be written in artistic writing called calligraphy.

Key vocabulary

99 names of God 99 characteristics of God used by Muslims to try to describe what God is like

shirk The Arabic word for the sin of worshipping anything other than God

tawhid Belief in the oneness of God

Check your understanding

1 Why did Muhammad's message about God cause conflict?

2 Explain three things that Muslims believe about God.

3 Explain what Muslims mean by 'tawhid'.

4 Explain what is meant by 'shirk'. Give examples.

5 'It is impossible to describe God.' Discuss this statement.

Who are the prophets in Islam?

The final and most important prophet in Islam is Muhammad, but who were the other prophets?

A prophet is someone who is believed to be a messenger sent by God. Muslims think that the prophets in Judaism and Christianity were sent by God to bring important messages to people on earth. The Qur'an mentions 25 prophets by name, including Abraham, Moses and Jesus. However, Muslims refer to the prophets by their Arabic names, so instead of Abraham, Moses and Jesus you will hear Muslims talk of Ibrahim, Musa and Isa. Muslims believe that this chain of prophets began with Adam in the Garden of Eden. Adam was both the first man and the first prophet. God spoke to him and soon his descendants began to spread over the whole earth.

Muslims believe that the Qur'an is the final and complete revelation from God. It does not contain a completely new message, though – it is a final, corrected, version of the inaccurately recorded teachings of previous prophets. For this reason, the Qur'an often includes additional or different detail when describing events that are also in the Bible.

Abraham (Ibrahim)

Abraham was born in the city of Ur in modern Iraq. At the time, the people of Ur believed in many gods, often linked to the environment. Many of their leaders also claimed that *they* were gods. However, the Qur'an says that Abraham rejected this, believing that there was only one God.

According to Islamic tradition, Abraham met Nimrod, the king of Babylon, who believed that he was a god. However, Nimrod was worried that he was losing power, as more and more of his people were starting to believe in one God. Nimrod wanted to debate with Abraham to show his people that he was a god and that Abraham was a liar. In surah 2 of the Qur'an, it says that Nimrod challenged Abraham's claim that only his God gives life and causes death by saying that he too can do this, perhaps by executing or freeing people. However, when Abraham said that his God makes the sun rise in the east and set in the west, Nimrod had no answer.

Jesus (Isa)

Jesus is viewed with great respect by Muslims and is an important prophet. There is a whole surah in the Qur'an that describes Jesus' miraculous birth to the virtuous virgin Mary. The Qur'an also tells of Jesus's miracles and teachings.

However, there is a significant difference between Muslim and Christian beliefs about Jesus. Muslims do not believe that Jesus died on a cross, but rather that God raised him to heaven alive. Muslims believe that the Qur'an corrects Christian misunderstandings about the nature of Jesus.

Fact

Muslims believe that Adam originally built the Ka'aba and it was later rebuilt by Abraham and his son Ishmael (Ismail). After this, it became misused as a place of pilgrimage for polytheists, who filled it with idols. Muslims believe that Muhammad reclaimed the Ka'aba as a place of worship to the one true God when he conquered Mecca.

Nimrod, the king of Babylon.

For Muslims, he is an important prophet who called people to submit to the one true God, but he is neither divine nor the Son of God, as Christians believe him to be.

Muhammad

Muhammad was born nearly 600 years after Jesus and a long time after Abraham and Moses. Although Muhammad was not divine, he is considered the most special of the prophets. He is often referred to as 'the Seal of all Prophets', or simply as 'the Prophet', to emphasise his importance as the final and most important of God's messengers.

Respecting the prophets

Most Muslims believe that it is disrespectful to show pictures of the prophets, particularly Muhammad. Instead, much Islamic artwork is based on geometric patterns and artistic writing called calligraphy. In a mosque, you will never see pictures of animals, people or God.

In the past, there was Islamic artwork showing the prophets. The first pictures were created by Muslim artists in the thirteenth century and were paid for by the rich and powerful people of the time. The pictures show almost every part of Muhammad's life recorded in the Qur'an. They were made for both Sunni and Shi'a worshippers and examples can be found in major museums and libraries around the world. Despite this, most Muslims in the twenty-first century believe it is wrong to create pictures of prophets.

Fact

In keeping with the tradition started by Abraham, Jews and Muslims **circumcise** boys at a young age. In Judaism, this happens after eight days. Muslim boys are usually circumcised before puberty. Muslims often name their children after prophets like Muhammad and Abraham, or other figures from Islamic history, such as the caliphs.

The inside of the Sheikh Lotfollah Mosque in Iran is decorated with calligraphy and geometric art.

Key vocabulary

circumcise To remove a male's foreskin

Check your understanding

1 How many prophets are mentioned in the Qur'an and who was the first?
2 What are the Arabic names given to Abraham, Moses and Jesus?
3 Explain why Nimrod wanted to debate with Abraham and what happened.
4 Explain the differences between Islamic and Christian beliefs about Jesus.
5 'Prophets should not be drawn.' Discuss this statement.

Unit 1: History and belief

What do Muslims believe happens when we die?

Muslims believe that those who please God will be accepted into paradise, but what will God's judgement be based on?

Heaven and hell

The question of what happens when we die has preoccupied people throughout history. Different religions attempt to answer this question in different ways. Muslims believe that human life is a gift from God, but also a test. They believe that when people die they wait in their graves until the **Day of Judgement**. On this day, God will judge all people who have ever lived and decide what happens to them in the afterlife. Muslims believe that, while people wait in their graves, God sends two angels to ask them about their beliefs and how they have lived. If people answer correctly, then they have a peaceful experience in the grave. If they answer incorrectly, they are tormented until the Day of Judgement.

Those who have fully submitted themselves to God will be rewarded with **Jannah** (paradise, heaven). Muslims believe that Jannah is beyond what humans can imagine, but the Qur'an likens it to a beautiful garden with four rivers of water, milk, honey and wine running through it. Nobody in Jannah will experience suffering. It will be a place of complete comfort and contentment, and people will never grow tired of it. In order to enter Jannah, people will have to cross a bridge. This will be easy for those who are destined for heaven, but those who are not will fall from the bridge and face terrible torments in the fires of **Jahannam** (hell).

Islamic artwork from the 14th century showing a paradise garden with a refreshing stream, flowering trees and birds.

Muslims believe that God wants everyone to enter Jannah, but people must choose whether to believe in one God, to accept the teachings of the Qur'an and to perform good acts, such as giving money to charity.

Muslims interpret the Qur'an's vivid descriptions of heaven and hell in different ways. Some think that the Qur'an should be understood literally. However, others think that it contains metaphors to describe a reality for which we do not have words. Non-Muslims might argue that the descriptions were simply to encourage people at the time of Muhammad to follow Islam through either fear of hell or the promise of many rewards in heaven. For example, the image of four rivers would have appealed to people living in a hot desert environment.

Hell and the Tree of Zaqqum

According to the Qur'an, the Tree of Zaqqum grows from the fire at the bottom of hell and its flowers are the heads of devils. Those in hell must eat the fruit of the tree, which makes their insides burn. The fires of hell are kept alight by burning bodies. When someone's skin is burned up, he or she is given new skin, which is then burned afresh. This happens for all eternity. The flames are hotter than any flame on earth and people will be in continual pain and misery.

An artist's depiction of the Tree of Zaqqum.

The Six Articles of Faith

Most Muslims think that getting to Jannah requires a mixture of good deeds and faith. Sunni Muslims believe that when Muhammad was asked about faith, he said that it involved six things. These are known as the Six Articles of Faith. They are:

- belief in God
- belief in angels
- belief in God's books (the Qur'an and other holy writings, some of which have been lost)
- belief in God's prophets
- belief in the Day of Judgement
- belief in God's plan.

> ❝ Those who believe and do good deeds will have an unfailing reward. ❞
> Qur'an 95:6–7

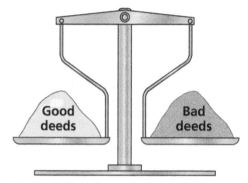

Muslims believe that everyone's actions will be weighed on the Day of Judgement.

The Day of Judgement

On the Day of Judgement, Muslims believe that all people will be judged on whether they have had faith and whether they have done good things on earth. Everyone is responsible for himself or herself and the actions of each person are weighed in a divine balance. Only God knows the minimum weight required to get into heaven, but good deeds count 10 times more than bad. Many Muslims do not think that all people in hell will be destined to remain there forever; because God is merciful, some people might enter heaven after being in hell.

Key vocabulary

Day of Judgement A day when all people's faith and deeds will be judged by God

Jahannam Hell

Jannah Paradise or heaven

Check your understanding

1 What do Muslims believe will happen on the Day of Judgement?

2 What are the Six Articles of Faith?

3 How does the Qur'an describe Jannah and Jahannam?

4 Explain how different Muslims might interpret the Qur'an's descriptions of Jannah and Jahannam.

5 'There is no life after death.' Discuss this statement, with reference to Islam.

Knowledge organiser

Key vocabulary

99 names of God 99 characteristics of God used by Muslims to try to describe what God is like

Allah The Arabic word for God

caliph The Arabic word for the leader of the whole Muslim community after the death of Muhammad; it literally means 'successor'. Sunni Muslims call the first four caliphs 'Rightly Guided Caliphs'

Caliphate The Islamic community ruled over by the caliph

circumcise To remove a male's foreskin

civil war A war between people of the same nation or region

Constitution of Medina The laws passed by Muhammad in Yathrib when he and his followers first settled there

Day of Judgement A day when all people's faith and deeds will be judged by God

hafiz Someone who has memorised the Qur'an (a man is a hafiz and a woman is called a hafiza)

Hijrah The migration of Muhammad and his followers to Yathrib (Medina) in 622 CE

idol A picture or object that people worship as part of their religion

Jahannam Hell

Jannah Paradise or heaven

Ka'aba A key holy site in Mecca; before Muhammad's time, this building contained 360 idols

Mecca A city in present-day Saudi Arabia; Muhammad was born here in 570 CE

Medina One of the main cities in Arabia in the time of Muhammad (originally called Yathrib); Muhammad and his followers fled here to escape persecution and create a new Muslim community

monotheism Belief in one God

mosque The place of worship for Muslims; it literally means 'place of prostration'

polytheism Belief in many gods

prophet A messenger of God

Qur'an The holy book of Islam, which Muslims believe contains the word of God; it literally means 'recitation'

Ramadan The ninth month of the Islamic year (which is based on the moon)

Revelation A message revealed by God to humans

Shi'a A minority group of Muslims who believe that Ali and his descendants should have succeeded Muhammad as leaders of Islam; the word means 'party of Ali'

shirk The Arabic word for the sin of worshipping anything other than God

Sunni The majority (about 85 per cent) of Muslims across the world who believe that the Rightly Guided Caliphs were rightful successors of Muhammad; the word means 'people of the tradition'

surah A chapter of the Qur'an; there are 114 surahs in total

tawhid Belief in the oneness of God

The Blue Mosque, Istanbul, Turkey.

Key facts

- Islam is the second-largest and fastest-growing religion in the world. It is a monotheistic faith that began in Arabia in the lifetime of the Prophet Muhammad, who was born in Mecca in 570 CE. Islam means 'submission' and Muslim means 'one who submits to God'.

- Muslims believe that Muhammad received revelations over 23 years from God about how people should live. The first revelation was received from the angel Jibril in 610 CE while Muhammad was praying in a cave. This event is known as the Night of Power. The revelations received by Muhammad were memorised by his followers and recorded in a book called the Qur'an after his death.

- Muhammad was a religious and political leader as well as a warrior who ruled first over Medina and then Mecca. He fought against persecution of early Muslims and by the end of his life was the most influential man in the Arabian Peninsula. He gained wide recognition as a prophet and brought previously warring tribes under Islamic rule.

- After Muhammad's death, Islam continued to spread under the rule of the caliphs, and a large Caliphate (empire) was established. However, there was disagreement amongst Muslims over who should succeed Muhammad as leader, which caused the religion to split into two groups: Sunni Muslims and Shi'a Muslims.

- Modern versions of the Qur'an are based on an official Qur'an compiled under the rule of the third caliph, Uthman. The Qur'an is written in Arabic and split into 114 surahs. It is believed to be the word of God and is treated with great respect by Muslims.

- Tawhid – the belief that God is one – is the most important Islamic belief. Anything that goes against tawhid is considered shirk. Muslims often describe God using 99 names, but ultimately Muslims believe that God is beyond anything that humans can describe or imagine.

- Muslims believe that Muhammad was the final prophet sent by God, but they believe God also revealed himself to earlier prophets mentioned in Jewish and Christian scriptures, like Adam, Abraham and Moses. Muslims believe that Jesus was a prophet, but think that viewing him as the Son of God is shirk.

- Muslims believe that there will be a Day of Judgement, when God will send people to paradise (Jannah) or hell (Jahannam) depending on their faith and deeds.

Key people

Abu Bakr The first Rightly Guided Caliph (632–634 CE) and Muhammad's closest companion

Abu Talib Muhammad's uncle

Ali The fourth Rightly Guided Caliph (656–661 CE) and Muhammad's cousin and son-in-law

Amina Muhammad's mother

Bilal A former slave who was one of Islam's first converts

Fatima Muhammad's daughter, who married Ali

Hussein Ali's son, who was killed in the Battle of Karbala

Ibrahim A prophet in Islam, known as Abraham in English.

Isa An important prophet in Islam; Jesus in English

Khadija A wealthy businesswoman and widow who became Muhammad's wife when she was 40 and was also the first to believe his message after the Night of Power

Muawiya The successor to Ali as the fifth caliph

Muhammad The final prophet, who received God's full revelation; he lived from 570–632 CE; Muslims will say or write PBUH after his name to show respect

Musa An important prophet in Islam; in English, Moses

Umar The second Rightly Guided Caliph (634–644 CE)

Uthman The third Rightly Guided Caliph (644–656 CE)

Islam in the modern world

In this book's second part, you will find out about how Muslims practise their religion in the modern world. You will explore the Five Pillars, which are central to life as a Muslim, and consider the challenges that Muslims face when following these today. You will also consider some of the most controversial questions people ask about Islam. Should women cover their bodies and faces? What is jihad? What is Islamophobia?

Unit 2: Islam in the modern world
The Five Pillars

What five practices are central to life as a Muslim?

In most religions, faith must be matched with action. It is not good enough just to know what the right thing to do is – you have to actually *do* it. Islam is no exception. The **Five Pillars** are five acts of worship that all Muslims are expected to do in their lives, if it is possible. They are called pillars because they help support a Muslim's faith; therefore, if one of the pillars collapses, his or her whole faith may fall with it. Sunni and Shi'a Muslims generally agree on the importance of these five acts.

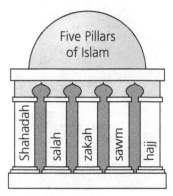

The Five Pillars of Islam.

1. The Shahadah (declaration of faith)

The **Shahadah** is the declaration of faith that there is only one God and that Muhammad is his messenger. This belief in the oneness of God (tawhid) is at the heart of Islam and was the reason why Muhammad and his followers were persecuted in its early years. The Shahadah is always recited in Arabic, the language of the Qur'an. A Muslim will say it thousands of time over the course of his or her lifetime as part of prayer. It is also whispered into the ears of children at birth and of Muslims at death.

> **Fact**
>
> Shi'a Muslims add Arabic words meaning 'Ali is the friend (*wali*) of God' to the first two parts of the Shahadah.

> **The Shahadah**
> 66 La ilaha illa Allah, Muhammad rasul Allah. 99
> This translate as: 'There is no god but God, and Muhammad is his messenger.'

2. Salah (prayer)

The Arabic word '**salah**' is usually translated as 'prayer', but it can also mean 'worship'. The Qur'an only mentions praying three times a day, but most Muslims pray five times. Muslims are not restricted to praying five times a day – they can pray to God anywhere at any time, for example, to ask God for help or to give him thanks. When praying informally, prayers are usually said in the language of the person praying rather than in Arabic.

3. Zakah (charity)

Each year, a Muslim must give 2.5 per cent of his or her savings to charity. This is called **zakah**. Muslims believe that their wealth is given to them by God and they therefore have a responsibility to share some of it with those who are less fortunate than themselves. 'Zakah' literally means 'that which purifies'. Muslims believe that zakah purifies the remainder of their money and prevents them from becoming greedy.

A Muslim woman praying.

4. Sawm (fasting during Ramadan)

'**Sawm**' is the Arabic term for fasting during the month of Ramadan, when the fast lasts from dawn to sunset. All Muslims are encouraged to fast, except those who are very young, very old, or who cannot fast for health reasons or other circumstances, such as travelling or being pregnant.

There are many spiritual benefits to fasting. Muslims feel a strong sense of the global Muslim community, the **ummah**, because everyone is fasting at the same time, and it helps them to consider the challenges faced by the poor. It is an extra test of self-control for Muslims living in Britain – unlike in Middle Eastern countries, the majority of the population is *not* fasting. A celebratory meal is often shared in the evenings, when the fast is over.

5. Hajj (pilgrimage to Mecca)

Every Muslim hopes that at some point in life he or she can make a **pilgrimage** to Mecca. This pilgrimage is called **hajj**. Each year, in the 12th month of the Islamic calendar, about three million pilgrims set off from different parts of the globe to reach Mecca and participate in the most spiritual of all journeys for a Muslim. It is a Muslim's duty to make this pilgrimage at least once, if they are physically able and wealthy enough to do so. Like fasting during Ramadan, Muslims think that the shared experience of hajj strengthens the ummah, as well as their own faith.

Millions of pilgrims visit the Ka'aba in Mecca every year.

Key vocabulary

Five Pillars Five important acts of worship in a Muslim's life, which form the basis of the faith

hajj A pilgrimage to Mecca

pilgrimage A journey taken to a place of religious importance

salah Prayers that Muslims must perform five times a day

sawm Fasting during the month of Ramadan

Shahadah The Muslim declaration of faith – there is no god but God, and Muhammad is his messenger

ummah The global community of Muslims

zakah The act of giving 2.5 per cent of your savings to charity

Fact

Before the invention of aeroplanes, many pilgrims would travel for years by foot or camel across Africa or Asia to reach Mecca. They would be greatly respected for doing so, and this achievement of completing hajj would be recognised by people gaining the status of hajji (a man) or hajja (a woman).

Check your understanding

1 What are the names of the Five Pillars of Islam?

2 How often do Muslims pray?

3 Which of the Five Pillars means literally 'that which purifies'? Why is this pillar important?

4 What do Muslims believe are the benefits of fasting?

5 Why do you think the Shahadah is the most important of the Five Pillars for Muslims?

Prayer and the mosque

How do Muslims pray, and what happens in a mosque?

The Shahadah (declaration of faith) is the most important of the Five Pillars. The second most important is salah – prayer five times a day. Salah provides an opportunity for Muslims to show submission – 'islam' to God. Prayers are always said in Arabic and usually happen at dawn, midday, mid-afternoon, dusk and evening. Prayers can be performed in any location, but whenever possible many Muslims choose to attend a mosque where the prayers are led by an imam (leader). The imam stands in front of others with his back to them while leading the prayers.

The only time when attending mosque is compulsory is for Friday noon prayers, and this only applies to men. Women are not required to attend, but if they do, they pray in a separate part of the mosque or behind the men. This is so that men are not distracted during prayer. On a Friday, the imam will deliver a sermon.

The five times a day when Muslims should pray are announced by a **muezzin** reciting the **adhan** (call to prayer). The muezzin can do this inside the mosque or from one of the mosque's towers, known as **minarets**. The adhan reminds Muslims of the key beliefs of Islam – there is no god but God, and Muhammad is his messenger.

A muezzin calling Muslims to prayer. Today, speakers are often used so that the adhan can be better heard.

Wudu

Before praying, Muslims must perform a ritual wash known as **wudu** . This involves washing hands, mouth, nostrils, face, arms, the top of the head and feet a specific number of times in a particular order. Most

The adhan (call to prayer)
❝ *Allahu akbar Allahu akbar* [said twice]
God is the greatest, God is the greatest
Ashhadu an lailaha illAllah [said twice]
I bear witness that there is no God but God
Ashhadu anna Muhammadan rasul Allah [said twice]
I bear witness that Muhammad is the Messenger of God
Hayya aala as-salah, hayya aala as-salah
Come to prayer, come to prayer
Hayya aala al-falah, hayya aala al-falah
Come to success, come to success
Allahu akbar, Allahu akbar
God is the greatest, God is the greatest
La ilaha illAllah
There is no God but God ❞

Activity

Listen to a call to prayer and see if you can follow the Arabic in the purple box below.

Fact

When entering a mosque, Muslims remove their shoes to show respect to God and keep the space clean. When Muslims perform salah outside of a mosque, they pray on a prayer mat to make sure that they are still praying somewhere clean. They will also remove their shoes before standing on the mat.

mosques have an area where people can perform this ritual. There are usually separate areas for men and women.

After washing, the person is ready to pray. This is done in the main prayer hall, which is found in all mosques. The word 'mosque' literally means 'place of prostration'. Unlike many other religious buildings, the main prayer room in a mosque does not contain seats, because Muslims need space to pray. As they pray, people perform a series of movements – for example, standing, bowing and **prostrating**.

When praying together, Muslims stand shoulder to shoulder to show that they are united and equal as part of the ummah. In mosques, there is usually an alcove in a wall called a **mihrab**, which points towards Mecca. Muslims always face in the direction of Mecca when they pray.

What do mosques look like?

As well as having minarets, it is common for mosques to have a dome. There are practical and religious reasons for this. In hot countries, the dome helps to keep the mosque cool. It also amplifies sound. However, it is also symbolic of God's rule over everything and of the worldwide ummah. The only piece of furniture normally found inside the prayer room of a mosque is a platform called a **minbar**. This is where the imam delivers his sermon.

There are approximately 1750 mosques in the UK today, but it is not always easy to spot them from the outside. This is because there is a mix of purpose-built mosques and houses, churches and other buildings that have been converted into mosques.

During prayer, Muslims perform a series of movements (rak'ah).

Some of the most architecturally impressive buildings in the world are mosques.

Fact

As well as a place to pray, Mosques are used as Madrassahs – places for children to learn Arabic and how to pray, and to memorise the Qur'an.

Activity

Imagine you have visited a mosque. Using all the key words on this page, write a diary entry explaining what you saw and why it was happening.

Key vocabulary

adhan The call to prayer

mihrab An alcove in a mosque wall showing the direction of Mecca

minaret A mosque tower on a mosque from which the muezzin traditionally gives the adhan

minbar A platform in a mosque from which the imam delivers his sermon

muezzin A person responsible for performing the adhan in a mosque

prostrating Bowing with part of the body above the knees touching the floor, such as the hands

wudu Ritual washing before prayer

Check your understanding
1. Why is prayer important to Muslims, and when and where is it done?
2. What is the role of the muezzin and the adhan?
3. What is wudu?
4. How do Muslims perform salah?
5. Describe the features that mosques often have in common.

Ramadan and Eid ul-Fitr

Why do Muslims fast during Ramadan, and what happens at Eid ul-Fitr?

What is Ramadan?

During the month of Ramadan, Muslims celebrate Muhammad receiving his first revelation from the angel Jibril on the Night of Power. This is believed to have happened towards the end of Ramadan. On this night, Muslims will often stay awake praying, as they believe that God is particularly merciful at this time.

Each year, during the 30 days of Ramadan, Muslims will not eat or drink between sunrise and sunset. This is called sawm – fasting – and is the fourth pillar of Islam. Fasting during this month is commanded in the Qur'an. Muslims think that fasting can provide spiritual strength and self-control over greed and other selfish instincts. It also helps develop compassion for people who are living in poverty, without enough food and drink, and helps increase people's gratitude for what they have. Last, Muslims believe that the fast helps strengthen the global community of Muslims, the ummah, because all Muslims are sharing in the same experience.

Not every Muslim is required to fast during Ramadan. People who are ill, pregnant, elderly or young (usually under about 12 years old) are not expected to fast. Soldiers and people who are travelling on long journeys are also permitted to miss the fast, but should make up the missed days at another time.

Muslims believe that if they do not live in a way that honours God during Ramadan, then their fast has no spiritual value. Muhammad is reported to have said: 'There are many who fast during the day and pray all night, but they gain nothing but hunger and sleeplessness.' As well as paying special attention to the way they treat others, Muslims might read the Qur'an or attend mosque more often during this month.

Ramadan is the ninth month of the Islamic year, which is based on the moon. This means that every year Ramadan occurs about 11 days earlier than the previous year. As such, the number of hours that Muslims are required to fast can vary greatly. In the summer months, the fast lasts longer than the winter months, when there are fewer hours of daylight. Going without food and water in the heat of summer can be especially difficult.

At the end each day of fasting, people may enjoy a large meal and celebrate the achievement of completing the fast. Often, families will also share a pre-fast meal together early in the morning before the fast begins. In the summer, there is not as long between the evening and morning meals, so the morning meal is quite light. In winter, the morning meal is eaten later, and so is generally more substantial.

> ### Fact
> Nothing is allowed to enter people's mouths while fasting. This means that people cannot smoke or chew gum. Even swallowing water while swimming is seen as breaking the fast.

The fast is usually broken by eating a date, as it is believed that this is how Muhammad broke his fast.

Fact

Muslims in very northerly or southerly parts of the world still have to fast from dawn until dusk. However, in very northern countries there may be very few or no hours of darkness during the summer. The Muslim community in Helsinki, Finland, for example, may be required to fast for 21 hours. When this happens, Muslims who live in such locations may follow the fasting times kept in Mecca, or in the nearest Muslim country.

Eid ul-Fitr

Ramadan ends with a three-day celebration known as **Eid ul-Fitr**, which begins on the first day of the 10th month of the year. Usually, on the first day of Eid ul-Fitr, Muslim families attend mosque to thank God that their fast is complete. They are reminded by the imam that Muhammad promised that those who complete the fast will receive both pleasure on earth and also a reward from God on the Day of Judgement.

Festivities to celebrate Eid ul-Fitr.

Eid ul-Fitr is a time of both prayer and celebration. Muslims will often decorate their houses, eat feasts together and give each other gifts and cards. It is also a popular time for Muslims to get married. In Muslim-majority countries, Eid is a public holiday like Christmas and Easter are in the UK. In countries where Islam is not the majority religion, Muslims will usually take time off work in order to celebrate Eid. Some employers may give Muslim employees a day off work.

Eid ul-Adha

During the 12th month of the Islamic year, Muslims have another celebration, called **Eid ul-Adha**, when the prophet Abraham's faith and obedience to God are remembered. Eid ul-Adha takes place at the end of the five days of hajj, but is celebrated by Muslims all around the world.

A carnival in Morocco to celebrate Eid ul-Adha.

Key vocabulary

Eid ul-Adha A four-day celebration in the final 12 month of the Islamic year

Eid ul-Fitr A three-day celebration after Ramadan

Check your understanding

1. What must Muslims do and not do during Ramadan?
2. Name three groups of people who do not have to fast.
3. Why do Muslims fast during Ramadan?
4. How are the dates of Ramadan decided and how does this affect those fasting?
5. Describe what happens at the end of the month of Ramadan.

What happens on hajj?

Hajj is a pilgrimage that every Muslim tries to undertake during the course of his or her lifetime, but what does this physical and spiritual journey involve?

Muhammad lived on the Arabian Peninsula, and this is where Muslims believe that he received the Qur'an. As you have seen, the city of Mecca has great significance in Islam, and it is here – and places nearby – that the Qur'an tells Muslims to visit. They must do this on a pilgrimage called hajj at least once in their life, if they are able.

In order for the pilgrimage to have spiritual value, pilgrims must not be in debt and must make sure their family is provided for while they are away. Certain people are not required to go on hajj – for example, people who are too old, poor or ill. One person can also go on hajj on behalf of others. The pilgrimage has to take place from 8 to 12 Dhul-Hijjah, the final month of the Islamic calendar. There are approximately three million pilgrims in Mecca during hajj.

The prophet's mosque

Before arriving in Mecca, many pilgrims visit the Prophet's Mosque in Medina to prepare themselves spiritually for hajj by praying. The mosque can hold almost 700,000 people. It contains the tomb of Muhammad and the first two caliphs, and is the second holiest site in the world for Muslims. Some Muslims choose to travel to Medina after, rather than before, completing hajj.

The Prophet's Mosque in Medina.

Ihram

When approaching Mecca, pilgrims must enter into a spiritual state of holiness or purity known as **ihram**. While in this state, pilgrims are not allowed to do various things, including smoke, shave, wear perfume or jewellery, or cut their nails. It is a time to focus wholly on God. At this time, all pilgrims wear the same white cotton clothing. Men usually wear one cotton sheet around their waist and one over their shoulder. Women wear a long white dress and head covering and do not cover their faces. The simple clothing worn by pilgrims is intended to show purity and humility before God, as well as equality between all people on hajj. It is also a reminder to pilgrims to focus on God rather than their everyday lives.

What happens in Mecca?

During hajj, some pilgrims stay in hotels, many stay in tents and others may simply sleep on roadsides. There are various tasks to be completed within the five days. With the high temperatures and with so many people in one place all trying to do the same things, this can be a challenge.

The simple clothing people wear in the state of ihram is a reminder to focus on God rather than everyday life.

On arriving in Mecca, pilgrims head towards the Grand Mosque, which is home to the Ka'aba. Pilgrims walk around the Ka'aba seven times in an anticlockwise direction. Those who can get close enough might try to touch or kiss it, but the mosque can hold millions of people and so not everyone has this opportunity.

After circling the Ka'aba, pilgrims walk or run back and forth between two hills, Marwah and Safa. Muslims believe that Abraham's wife rushed between these two hills in search of water for her dehydrated son, Ishmael. Travelling between the hills also symbolises the desperate search of the pilgrims' souls to find God. In the past, this took place outdoors, but now there are two long air-conditioned corridors.

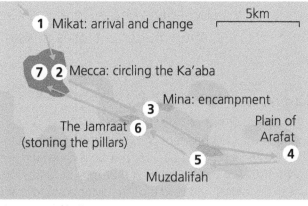

The stages of hajj.

During hajj, pilgrims stand on or near Mount Arafat from noon to sunset, praying for forgiveness from God. This is a significant location, because it is believed to be where God forgave Adam and Eve after they disobeyed him by eating fruit from a tree that was forbidden to them, and also where Muhammad delivered his final sermon. Many pilgrims describe a feeling of freedom and joy as they receive God's forgiveness for everything they have done wrong.

After Mount Arafat, pilgrims collect stones and head to Mina to throw the stones at three pillars, which represent Satan. This is done to remember the willingness of the prophet Abraham to sacrifice his son, Ishmael, despite Satan telling him not to. It also symbolises Muslims' own rejection of evil. The stoning of Satan is often followed by the open-air sacrifice of an animal such as a goat or sheep. The meat can be eaten in Mina, but is often frozen and sent to poor Muslims in other countries.

At the end of hajj, pilgrims leave the state of ihram, and men will join a queue outside one of Mecca's many barber shops to have their heads shaved. Women usually just have one lock of their hair removed. Finally, pilgrims complete their pilgrimage by returning to the Ka'aba and circling it seven more times.

Fact

In 2015, it is estimated that approximately 2000 people died in a stampede while throwing stones at Satan. In response to this tragedy, all pilgrims were given electronic GPS bracelets to wear in 2016, and 1000 cameras were installed at holy sites to alert organisers of overcrowding.

Activity

Write a travel guide for hajj, giving advice on how to prepare, what will happen and why, and explaining what Muslims believe are the benefits of this pilgrimage.

Key vocabulary

ihram The state of holiness or purity entered into by pilgrims before beginning hajj

Check your understanding

1 Who is and who is not required to go on hajj?
2 When does hajj take place and how might a Muslim prepare for it?
3 Explain what Muslims do and do not do while in the state of ihram and why.
4 Describe what happens on hajj and explain why these things are done.
5 'All religious people should go on pilgrimage.' Discuss this statement.

Sunni and Shi'a Islam

What are the similarities and differences between Sunni and Shi'a Muslims, and what effect does this have in the modern world?

Similarities

Today, the majority of Muslims – about 85 per cent – are Sunni. In Britain, approximately 95 per cent of Muslims are Sunni. Although Sunni and Shi'a Muslims disagree over who should have succeeded Muhammad (see pages 100–101), there is much that they do agree on. Both groups believe that there is only one God and that Muhammad was his final prophet. They both use the Qur'an as the basis of their beliefs and they both follow the Five Pillars, although Shi'a Muslims have other practices that they believe are similarly important. Both Sunni and Shi'a Muslims attend mosque to pray at noon on a Friday, although they use a slightly different adhan and different prayer positions. The Qur'an only specifies praying three times a day, so some Shi'a Muslims combine the five daily prayers into three sets of prayers.

When Muslims first moved to Britain, Sunni and Shi'a Muslims would often share the same places to pray, but as Islam grew in Britain this became less common and the different branches of Islam developed their own identities.

> **Fact**
>
> The largest form of Shi'a Islam is known as Twelver Shi'a, but there are other types of Shi'a Islam: the Isma'ilis (Seveners) and the Zaydis (Fivers). These groups are given their names because of their differing beliefs about how many imams followed Muhammad.

Differences

Sunni Muslims believe that the Qur'an, **Hadith** (the reported teachings of Muhammad) and Sunnah (the example of Muhammad) show them how to live. These three sources form the basis of **Shari'a law**, which provides guidance on all aspects of life.

Shi'a Muslims believe that God did not want to leave his people without a spiritual leader on earth, so he chose 12 **imams** – Ali and his descendants. God gave the imams the ability to be examples for Muslims, leading them in all aspects of life and showing them the truth that they should follow. Shi'a Muslims believe that in 874 CE, when the 12th imam was six years old, God took him into hiding to avoid him being killed as the previous imams had been. They think that he will return at the end of time, along with Jesus, to bring peace and justice to earth.

The site of a suicide car bomb in Karbala, Iraq, during a Shi'a pilgrimage.

Both Sunni and Shi'a Muslims celebrate Ramadan, Eid ul-Fitr and Eid ul-Adha, but they remember different events during the Islamic festival of Ashura.

Iraqi Shi'a men beating themselves with chains to remember the assassination of Ali's son, Hussein.

Sunni Muslims remember the prophet Noah leaving the ark and Moses being freed from the Egyptians, while Shi'a Muslims mourn the death of Ali's son Hussein, who was beheaded during the Battle of Karbala (in present-day Iraq). During this festival, Shi'as often wear dark clothes, blacken their faces and bodies, and beat their chests with their fists to show their sorrow. In countries such as Pakistan and India, some men even cut themselves with knives, chains and blades to draw blood and suffer as Hussein did.

Shari'a Law

Shari'a Law teaches Muslims what is **halal**. '*Halal*' is an Arabic word meaning 'permitted'. The word is most often heard when describing food, but it can also be used to describe prayer, fasting, clothes or other things – any object or action can be halal. The opposite of halal is **haram**, which means 'unlawful' or 'forbidden'. Any meat that Muslims eat must be halal. For meat to be halal, the animal needs to be killed by cutting the jugular vein, carotid artery and windpipe with a sharp knife. All blood is then drained from the animal. During this process, an Islamic blessing is recited. Muslims believe that eating pork and drinking alcohol is always haram.

There are many halal butchers and restaurants in the UK.

Modern clashes

Many Muslims accept that both Sunni and Shi'a Islam are valid forms of their religion, but there have been conflicts between the two groups, which continue today. There are many reasons for clashes between Sunnis and Shi'as. In Iraq, there has been much violence between Sunni and Shi'a Muslims caused by historical, religious and political factors. For example, in 2007, at a popular time of Shi'a pilgrimage to Karbala in Iraq, a car bomb was set off near a Shi'a mosque. Approximately 60 people were killed and about 150 more were injured. Violence erupted on the streets and there were many shootings.

Key vocabulary

Ashura A festival in which Shi'a Muslims mourn the death of Ali's son Hussein at the Battle of Karbala

Hadith The reported sayings of Muhammad, heard by people during his life and written down in the centuries after his death

halal Permitted

haram Forbidden

imam A word used by Shi'a Muslims to refer to Ali and his 11 descendants. It also means the leader of prayers in a Sunni mosque

Shari'a law Guidance on all aspects of life for Muslims, from the three main sources of authority – the Qur'an, Sunnah and Hadith

Check your understanding

1 Which is the largest branch of Islam in the world?
2 In a table, show the similarities and differences between Sunni and Shi'a Muslims.
3 Explain what is meant by Shar'ia Law and how it helps Muslims?
4 What is halal food?
5 Explain the significance of the festival of Ashura to different Muslims.

Unit 2: Islam in the modern world
What should women wear?

Why does the issue of what Muslim women wear cause controversy amongst both Muslims and non-Muslims?

The Qur'an teaches that both men and women should dress modestly. This is interpreted in different ways by different Muslims. Some believe it means that women should wear a **hijab** – a scarf that covers some or all of the head. Other Muslims believe that dressing modestly means wearing a **niqab** – a cloth that covers the whole face except the eyes. There are also Muslims who believe that to dress modestly means women wearing a **burqa** – a garment that covers the body from head to toe, often with a mesh screen to see through. In most Islamic countries, the hijab is considered sufficient. However, there are also Muslims who choose not to wear any religious covering at all.

Recently, some European countries have banned Muslim women from wearing religious coverings in public. This has caused much controversy. Some of the arguments that are made by both sides are explained below. Some people believe that all religious coverings are wrong, while others are just against the niqab or burqa, but not the hijab.

Arguments for banning coverings

Those who do not support women wearing a covering sometimes claim that women are forced to wear these garments by their husbands or fathers against their own will. This is considered oppressive and as evidence that women are seen as inferior by male Muslims. People argue that wearing a covering belongs to a different time, when people had different views from those found in modern Europe. They say that we now live in more forward-looking and **secular** societies.

Some people also argue that wearing a covering like the niqab stops Muslim women from integrating into European societies. They see it as a sign of separation that sends a message to non-Muslims that they are different. This makes it more difficult for Muslims and non-Muslims to have a positive relationship. Some people simply say that they think covering the head or body is impolite or that it frightens them in some way.

Sometimes the media have used images of women wearing a niqab when reporting on acts of terrorism carried out by other people claiming to be Muslims. Some newspapers have done this when the act was not carried out by people wearing any covering. This sort of treatment of Islam may make people link the idea of covering one's body with terrorism, so they feel threatened by it.

Arguments against banning coverings

On the other hand, many Muslim women say that covering their hair, face or body is something that they have chosen to do – men have not made them do so. They argue that religious freedom means women have the right to wear a covering if they choose.

> ### Fact
> Most Muslims think that men should be covered from the navel to the knees, but there are also countries where it would be considered immodest for a man to wear shorts and show his bare legs.

A woman wearing a hijab.

A woman wearing a niqab.

A woman wearing a burqa.

Some Muslim women argue that wearing a covering maintains their dignity; it allows them to be respected. It stops them from being simply an object to which men are attracted. It focuses men's attention on what is most important – the quality of a woman's character – rather than external beauty. They say that real freedom and equality means making it possible for women to be respected while covering themselves. Coverings, they may argue, also free women from having to spend time making themselves look a certain way in an attempt to meet the expectations of what society says is attractive.

Some people argue that wearing a covering does not encourage separation between Muslims and non-Muslims. Rather, it gives freedom to Muslim women to take part in society without compromising their beliefs or abandoning their identity as a Muslim, which could cause them to lose the respect of others in their community. An example of this is wearing a **burkini**.

A burkini is a type of swimsuit that covers most of the body. In 2016, it was banned in some places in France, and women who continued to wear it were fined.

Feminist attitudes

Some **feminists** are critical of what they see as **patriarchal** attitudes in Muslim-majority countries in parts of the Middle East. For example, in Saudi Arabia, women can be punished for not covering their heads and bodies. It is also illegal for women to drive in Saudi Arabia. Feminists also criticise the practice of polygamy (men having more than one wife), which is legal in some Islamic countries. The Qur'an permits a man to have up to four wives if he can treat each wife equally. Like many Arabian men of his time, Muhammad is thought to have had 12 wives, including Khadija. However, many people believe that this is an outdated and unfair practice that should not be permitted in the modern world.

Key vocabulary

burkini Swimwear worn by Muslim women to maintain modesty; it was banned in 20 French towns in 2016

burqa A cloak that covers the body from head to toe, often with a mesh screen to see through

feminist Someone who argues for women's rights and believes women are not being treated equally

hijab A scarf that covers some or all of the head and hair, but not the face

niqab A cloth that covers the head and face, except the eyes

patriarchal A word used to describe a society where men have more power and control than women

secular Non-religious

Check your understanding
1. What does the Qur'an teach about how Muslims should dress?
2. What is the difference between a hijab, niqab and burqa?
3. Explain two arguments for, and two arguments against, banning religious coverings.
4. Explain why feminists might be critical of what happens in some Islamic countries.
5. 'Religious clothing should not be worn publicly in the UK.' Discuss this statement.

What is jihad?

The Arabic word 'jihad' literally means 'to struggle' and can refer to a physical or a spiritual struggle. How has jihad been interpreted and carried out throughout the centuries?

Lesser jihad

In the years following the Night of Power, Muhammad and his followers were persecuted because of their monotheistic message. The polytheistic tribes who lived in Mecca, including the Quraysh tribe, used violence to prevent Muhammad from preaching. As a result, Muhammad and his followers fled from Mecca to Medina, where they established the first Islamic community.

While in Medina, the Qur'an continued to be revealed to Muhammad. The revelations he received included practical matters, such as how the new community should work and what laws its people should follow. As Muhammad was establishing his new community in Medina, he and his followers were attacked. The revelations received during this time explained when fighting should and should not happen.

Muslims believe that passages of the Qur'an such as the one above show that fighting was an acceptable means of self-defence for the early Muslim community in Medina. Islam could have been wiped out if Muhammad and his persecuted followers did not fight in order to preserve their religion. However, Muhammad and his followers did not just fight in self-defence – they also fought to help spread the message of Islam. It was not unusual to go to war in order to gain power at this time. The Mesopotamians, Greeks and Romans all fought against others to extend their political power.

> 66 They ask you [Prophet] about fighting in the sacred month. Say, 'Fighting in that month is a great offence, but to bar others from God's path, to disbelieve in Him, prevent access to the Sacred Mosque, and expel its people, are still greater offences in God's eyes: persecution is worse than killing.' 99
>
> Qur'an 2:217

By the time of Muhammad's death, Muslims had conquered the whole of Arabia, and within a century of his death Muhammad's followers had carried his message to Syria, Iraq, Jerusalem and further west into Egypt and North Africa, establishing a large Islamic Caliphate or empire. By 750 CE, the Caliphate stretched from the westernmost point of Spain to the western edge of India.

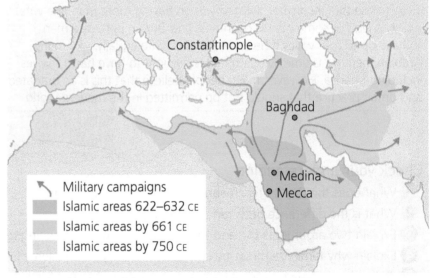

Military campaigns
Islamic areas 622–632 CE
Islamic areas by 661 CE
Islamic areas by 750 CE

A map showing some of the areas under Islamic rule by 750 CE.

Islamic militancy today

The majority of people today believe that people should be free to choose their religion (or no religion), rather than having a particular religion forced upon them. The majority of Muslims also believe that using violence to spread Islam is unacceptable. However, groups of Islamic **militants** such as Al-Qaeda, Boko Haram and Islamic State in Iraq and Syria (also called ISIS or Daesh) disagree. They believe Jews, Christians and other Muslims are guilty of shirk and use the Arabic word *'kafir'* to identify them as 'unbelievers' who need to be killed. Such groups want to set up an Islamic Caliphate in Syria and Iraq, free from what they see as 'impure' Western influences.

Muslims protesting against the use of their religion to justify acts of terrorism.

On 11 September 2001, two aeroplanes were hijacked by Al-Qaeda and flown into the World Trade Center in New York, killing nearly 3000 people. Since then, there have been many more terrorist attacks by Islamic militants, including bombings in London in 2005 and Paris in 2015. The vast majority of Muslims are appalled by the actions of these groups and reject both their violent interpretation of the Qur'an and also their attitude towards people of different religions.

Greater jihad

Most Muslims today interpret jihad as either a spiritual struggle inside oneself or as a fight against injustice rather than a physical struggle against an enemy. They point to a difference in what they call 'lesser jihad' and 'greater jihad'. Lesser jihad is the physical struggle to defend Islam. The *greater* jihad is to struggle against unfairness in the world and selfish desires within everyone, by following the teachings of Muhammad. An example of this struggle might be fasting during the month of Ramadan, saving money to give to the poor or speaking out against unfairness in the world.

Key vocabulary

jihad Literally, 'struggle'; this can be physical or spiritual

militants Individuals or groups who use violence to spread their ideas

Check your understanding

1. Why were Muhammad and the early Muslims persecuted?
2. Why did Muhammad and the early Muslims fight?
3. Explain what Islamic militant groups believe.
4. What do the majority of Muslims think about the views and actions of Islamic militants?
5. Using examples, explain what is meant by 'lesser' and 'greater' jihad.

Islam in Britain

Muslims make up approximately 5 per cent of the total population of Britain today. When did Muslims start living in Britain and what is life like for them today?

Islam arrives in Britain

When the Second World War ended in 1945, Britain ruled over a large empire that included the countries we now call India, Pakistan and Bangladesh. The British government invited people living in the empire to move to Britain in order to help rebuild the country. Many Muslims in Britain today are these people and their descendants. In recent decades, many Muslims have moved to Britain to escape persecution or violence in countries such as Somalia, Afghanistan, Iraq and Iran. There are also many white Muslims who were originally from Eastern Europe, as well as a small number of people who have converted to Islam from Christianity or no faith. This means that there is no such thing as a 'typical' Muslim, just as there is no such thing as a typical Jew, Christian or atheist.

Different groups of Muslims share many beliefs. However, there are also some differences and disagreements about what it means to be a Muslim in Britain. One of the reasons for this is that each community has brought parts of its own national identity or culture with it. These cultural differences affect the way in which Muslims practise their religion. Muslims from Pakistan or Iraq may have a different understanding of Islam from Muslims from Bosnia or Bangladesh. For example, they may disagree about whether women should cover their heads in public.

Muslims work in a variety of jobs in Britain. Many are successful athletes and some have represented Britain in sports such as cricket and athletics. Others have become successful business leaders, comedians, musicians, doctors, lawyers and politicians.

> ### Fact
> Although most Muslims started moving to Britain in the second half of the twentieth century, a few hundred Muslims lived in sixteenth-century Elizabethan England. One of Queen Elizabeth's favourite servants was a young Muslim girl who advised her on shoe fashion.

In 2016, Londoners voted for Sadiq Khan to be the first Muslim mayor of London.

Modern challenges

Since the terrorist attacks on the USA by Islamic militants in 2001, many Muslims living in mainly Christian or secular societies have experienced rising levels of **Islamophobia**. This situation has worsened in recent years because of other terrorist attacks. Some people argue that poor reporting of Islam in the media has further encouraged negative stereotypes and discrimination. They say that it is unfair to judge the majority of peace-loving Muslims on the violent actions of a small group and that these militants' actions are against the message of Islam.

Many people think that negative coverage of Islam in the media is one reason for the rise of Islamophobia.

Islamophobia

The word 'Islamophobia' is a neologism – a new word or expression that has entered the English language. 'Phobia' means either a fear or dislike of something. Islamophobia describes the way in which some people dislike, discriminate and are prejudiced against, Muslims because of their religion.

In recent years, there has been an increase in Islamophobic crime in Britain. This can involve verbal, physical or online abuse of Muslims. However, some people dislike the word 'Islamophobia', and argue that it may prevent people from making fair criticisms of Islam. For example, if someone says that it is wrong for women to be made to wear headscarves in conservative Islamic countries, he or she may be accused of being 'Islamophobic'. However, critics say that in free societies all religions and beliefs should be debated and that criticising a religion is not the same as making generalisations about whole groups of people.

Other challenges

Followers of a minority religion often live in the same area. There are many practical reasons for this. It is convenient for Muslims to live in an area where there is a mosque and other amenities, such as halal butchers and restaurants. However, this can limit the number of areas where Muslims might choose to live.

At some schools in Britain, like this primary school in London, the majority of pupils are Muslims.

In Muslim-majority countries, it is usual for men pray at the mosque at noon on Friday. However, in Britain, this can be difficult if someone has a job that requires him or her to be working at this time. Equally, in many Muslim-majority countries, there are public holidays during the month of Ramadan, but this is not the case in the UK. This means that people have to attend work or school while fasting.

When sending children to school in Britain, Muslim parents might be keen to ensure that they will be able to eat halal food and that the sports kit they wear is modest. They might also be concerned that the pull of secular ideas and lifestyles could cause their children to take Islam less seriously, or even abandon it. In some communities, it could bring shame on a family if a child abandoned the family's faith. This could cause children to feel like they have betrayed their culture or let their parents down.

In a multi-faith society, a Muslim may wish to marry someone of a different religion, against his or her parents' wishes. This could cause conflict in a family and difficulties for the couple when choosing a location to get married. Living different religious lives and deciding in which religion to bring up their own children could also cause problems. For the children, it could be confusing knowing which religion, if any, they should follow.

Key vocabulary

Islamophobia A word meaning 'a fear or dislike of Muslims'; disliking and discriminating against Muslims because of their religion

Check your understanding

1. What percentage of the British population are Muslims?
2. How has Islam become the second-largest religion in the UK?
3. What might Muslims in Britain disagree about and why?
4. What is Islamophobia and why do some people dislike the term?
5. 'Islamophobia is the main challenge facing Muslims in Britain today.' Discuss this statement.

Unit 2: Islam in the modern world
Knowledge organiser

Key vocabulary

adhan The call to prayer

Ashura A festival in which Shi'a Muslims mourn the death of Ali's son Hussein at the Battle of Karbala

burkini Swimwear worn by Muslim women to maintain modesty; it was banned in 20 French towns in 2016

burqa A cloak that covers the body from head to toe, often with a mesh screen to see through

Eid ul-Adha A four-day celebration in the final month of the Islamic year

Eid ul-Fitr A three-day celebration after Ramadan

feminist Someone who argues for women's rights and believes women are not being treated equally

Five Pillars Five important acts of worship in a Muslim's life, which form the basis of the faith

Hadith The reported sayings of Muhammad, heard by people during his life and written down in the centuries after his death

hajj A pilgrimage to Mecca

halal Permitted

haram Forbidden

hijab A scarf that covers some or all of the head and hair, but not the face

ihram The state of holiness or purity entered into by pilgrims before beginning hajj

imam A word used by Shi'a Muslims to refer to Ali and his 11 descendants. It also means the leader of prayers in a Sunni mosque

Islamophobia A word meaning 'a fear or dislike of Muslims'; disliking and discriminating against Muslims because of their religion

jihad Literally, 'struggle'; this can be physical or spiritual

mihrab An alcove in a mosque wall showing the direction of Mecca

militants Individuals or groups who use violence to spread their ideas

minaret A mosque tower from which the muezzin traditionally gives the adhan

minbar A platform in a mosque from which the imam delivers his sermon

muezzin A person responsible for performing the adhan in a mosque

niqab A cloth that covers the head and face except the eyes

patriarchal A word used to describe a society where men have more power and control than women

pilgrimage A journey taken to a place of religious importance

prostrating Bowing with part of the body above the knees touching the floor, e.g. hands

salah Prayers that Muslims must perform five times a day

sawm Fasting during the month of Ramadan

secular Non-religious

Shahadah The Muslim declaration of faith – there is no god but God, and Muhammad is his messenger

Shari'a law Guidance on all aspects of life for Muslims, from the three main sources of authority – the Qur'an, Sunnah and Hadith

ummah The global community of Muslims

wudu Ritual washing before prayer

zakah The act of giving 2.5 per cent of your savings to charity

Key facts

- There are five practices, known as the Five Pillars of Islam, that are central to life as a Muslim. The first and most important is the Shahadah (declaration of faith).

- The second pillar is salah (prayer five times a day). In mosques, a muezzin gives the adhan from either inside the mosque or from one of the minarets so that people know it is time to pray. Muslims perform wudu (washing) before praying and pray facing the direction of Mecca.

- During the month of Ramadan, Muslims fast from sunrise to sunset. The 30 days of fasting are followed by a celebration called Eid ul-Fitr. Those who are ill, elderly, young, pregnant or travelling do not have to fast.

- Hajj is a pilgrimage to Mecca that every Muslim tries to undertake during the course of his or her lifetime. Before arriving in Mecca, pilgrims enter the state of ihram and wear white cotton clothes. In order to become a hajji or hajja, pilgrims must circle the Ka'aba, walk or run between the hills of Marwah and Safa, pray for forgiveness on Mount Arafat and stone Satan at Mina. Approximately three million Muslims go on hajj each year. The pilgrimage lasts for five days in the last month of the Islamic year.

- Despite many similarities, Sunni and Shi'a Muslims have different beliefs and practices. Over the course of history, there have been violent clashes between Sunni and Shi'a Muslims, and these continue today.

- Shari'a law (based on the Qur'an, Hadith and Sunnah) teaches Muslims what is halal (permitted). Anything that is not halal is haram (forbidden).

- The question of whether Muslim women should wear a hijab, niqab, burqa or burkini causes much controversy, both within and outside Islam.

- The majority of Muslims view jihad (which means struggle) as a personal struggle to live a good life as a Muslim (the 'greater jihad'). They condemn the views and actions of Islamic militants.

- Five per cent of people in Britain follow Islam. There were some Muslims in Elizabethan England, but most moved to Britain in the second half of the twentieth century. Muslims in Britain today face a number of challenges, including Islamophobia.

Muslims celebrating Eid ul-Fitr.

Index

Abdullah 96
abortion 38
Abraham 10, 12, 13, 19, 26–7, 32, 34, 40, 42, 46, 94, 106–7, 111, 119, 121
Abrahamic faiths 13
Abu Bakr 97, 98, 100–1, 111
Abu Talib 96, 101, 111
Adam 78, 106, 111, 121
adhan (call to prayer) 116, 117, 130
Adrian IV, Pope 62
Al-Aqsa Mosque 15, 44
Al-Qaeda 127
Ali 97, 100, 101, 111, 123
Allah 94, 95, 110
Alpha 75
Amina 96, 111
Amish 66–7, 69
angels 108, 109
animal sacrifice 121
anti-Semitism 40, 41, 45, 47
anti-Zionism 45
Apocrypha 82, 83, 88
Arab tribes 96
Arabia 94, 96, 99, 111, 126
Arabian Peninsula 96, 99, 100, 111, 120
Arabic language 102
Arafat, Mount 121
Archbishop of Canterbury 74, 76, 88, 89
Arian controversy 59
Arius 59, 69
ark 18, 19, 22, 26, 27, 31
Ark of the Covenant 14, 15, 22
art, Islamic 105, 107
Ashura 123, 130
atheists 34, 35, 42, 47, 76, 77, 88
Augustine 69, 74, 89

Auschwitz 40, 41
authoritative 72, 73, 88

Babylonian exile 14, 15, 23
Babylonians 14, 27, 40
Badr, battle of 99
Baghdad, Iraq 87
baptism 59, 61, 68, 75, 346
Bar Mitzvah 35, 46, 47
Bat Mitzvah 35, 46, 47
ben Kosiba, Shimeon (Bar Kokhba) 17
Berkovits, Eliezer 42, 47
Bible 53, 66–7, 72–3, 80–3, 88, 94, 102, 106
  authors 72
  battle for the 73
  Catholic 72
  devil in the 82, 83
  earliest copy 72
  and gender equality 78–9
  as infallible 73
  interpretation 73, 88
  Protestant 72
  translations 64
  see also New Testament; Old Testament
Bilal 98, 111
bimah 22, 23, 26, 31
birth rituals 34, 46
Bishop of Rome 59, 60
bishops 59, 68, 69, 78
Black Death 40, 83
Boko Haram 85
Booth, William 65, 69
Britain 44, 74–5, 78, 128–9
Buddhism 87
burials 36, 46, 57
burkini 125, 130
burqa 124, 125, 130

Caliphate 100–1, 110–11, 126–7
caliphs 100–1, 110–11, 120
calligraphy 105, 107
Canterbury Cathedral 74
cantors 22
cardinals 62, 63, 68, 69, 78
catacombs 57, 68
Catherine of Aragon 64
Catholic Bible 72
Catholic Church 53, 60–1, 64, 69, 78
Catholicism 60–3, 69, 80, 87
censorship 76
census 75, 88
challah 31, 35
Charismatic Christianity 84–5, 88
charity 80
Christian Bible 102
Christian Church 59, 60–1, 69
  see also Catholic Church; Church of England; Early Church; Eastern Orthodox Church
Christianity 13, 27, 40, 49–89, 94, 96, 98–9, 105–7
  beginnings of 52, 54–5, 69
  Britain and 74–5
  Charismatic 84–5, 88
  and Constantine 58–9
  and the Crusades 81, 88
  definition 52–3
  denominations 53, 65–6, 68, 69
  Early Church 56–8, 57, 62, 66, 68, 69, 72
  festivals 74
  and the Great Schism 60–1, 69
  history of 50–69
  legalisation 59
  liberal 73, 75, 88
  and life after death 53, 54

Acknowledgements

Text

p43 Anne Frank – 'THE DIARY OF A YOUNG GIRL: THE DEFINITIVE EDITION by Anne Frank, edited by Otto H Frank and Mirjam Pressler, translated by Susan Massotty (Viking, 1997) copyright © The Anne Frank-Fonds, Basle, Switzerland, 1991. English translation copyright © Doubleday a division of Bantam Doubleday Dell Publishing Group Inc, 1995.; p77 Giles Fraser quotation, courtesy of Guardian News & Media Ltd; p77 Terry Sanderson quotation, courtesy of BBC News Online 22/11/2015; p77 John Hegarty quotation, courtesy of Guardian News & Media Ltd; p85, courtesy of Holy See Press Office; p86, Lord Sacks quotation, Open Parliament Licence; Extracts from the Good News Bible © 1994, published by the Bible Societies/HarperCollinsPublishers Ltd UK, reproduced with permission; QUR'AN BILINGUAL, REVISED EDITION translated by M.A.S. Abdel Haleem (2010). Used with permission of Oxford University Press.

Photographs

Cover and title page bogdan ionescu/Shutterstock, Dewitt/Shutterstock, Zoran Karapancev/Shutterstock, p7 bogdan ionescu/Shutterstock, pp8–9 Yadid Levy/Alamy Stock Photo, p11 mikhail/Shutterstock, p12 Lebrecht Music&Arts Photo Library/Alamy Stock Photo, p13 Prisma Archivo/Alamy Stock Photo, p14 DEA/A/Dagli orti/Getty Images, p15 Karol Koziowski/Shutterstock, p16 t Zvonimir Atletic/Shutterstock, p16 b robertharding/Alamy Stock Photo, p17 paul prescott/Shutterstock. Inc, p18 Matt Ragen/Shutterstock, p19 t robertharding/Alamy Stock Photo, p19 b Culture Club/Getty Images, p20 ChameleonsEye/Shutterstock, p21 TravelCollection/Alamy Stock Photo, p22 railway fx/Shutterstock, p23 Scythian/Shutterstock, p24 t Kobby Dagan/Shutterstock, p24 b imageBroker/Alamy Stock Photo, p25 t david156/Shutterstock, p25 b Anneka/Shutterstock, p27 dominique landau/Shutterstock, pp28–29 Zoonar GmbH/Alamy Stock Photo, p30 PhotoAlto sas/Alamy Stock Photo, p31 t S1001/Shutterstock, p31 b Robert Gray/Alamy Stock Photo, p32 Gregory Gerber/Shutterstock, p33 t ChameleonsEye/Shutterstock, p33 c Madlen/Shutterstock, p33 b supercat/Shutterstock, p34 ChameleonsEye/Shutterstock, p35 Rodolfo Arpia/Alamy Stock Photo, p36 t Robert Mulder/Alamy Stock Photo, p36 b a katz/Shutterstock, p37 Ira Berger/Alamy Stock Photo, p38 RosaireneBetancourt 9/Alamy Stock Photo, p39 Jack Guez/AFP/Getty Images, p40 t Lanmas/Alamy Stock Photo, p40 b Galerie Bilderwelt/Getty Images, p41 Campaign Against Antisemitism, p42 t Sean Gallup/Getty Images, p42 b American Jewish Archive, p43 Pictorial Press Ltd/Alamy Stock Photo, p47 ASAP/Alamy Stock Photo, p49 Dewitt/Shutterstock, pp50–51 Frank Gaertner/Shutterstock, p55 t Melvin Longhurst/Alamy Stock Photo, p55 b Joseph Clemson 1/Alamy Stock Photo, p56 t North Wind Picture Archives/Alamy Stock Photo, p56 b Universal History Archive/Getty Images, p57 imageBroker/Alamy Stock Photo, p58 t Aleks49/Shutterstock, p58 b Butterfly Hunter/Shutterstock, p59 Kean Collection/Archive Photos/Getty Images, p60 t Aurelian Images/Alamy Stock Photo, p60 b Mi.Ti/Shutterstock, p61 germip/Shutterstock, p62 t epa european pressphoto agency b.v./Alamy Stock Photo, p62 b Chris Hellier/Alamy Stock Photo, p63 t Evocation Images/Shutterstock, p63 b Alessandra Benedetti/Corbis via Getty Images, p64 t Prisma Archivo/Alamy Stock Photo, p64 b Pictorial Press Ltd/Alamy Stock Photo, p65 Anna Yu/Alamy Stock Photo, p66 Roman Babakin/Shutterstock, p67 t George Sheldon/Shutterstock.Inc, p67 b Stock Connection Blue/Alamy Stock Photo, p68 MSE Stock/Alamy Stock Photo, p69 Prisma Archivo/Alamy Stock Photo, pp70–71 Ken Hawkins/Alamy Stock Photo, p72 t Chimpinski/Shutterstock, p72 b www.BibleLandPictures.com/Alamy Stock Photo, p73 The Print Collector/Alamy Stock Photo, p74 t PjrWindows/Alamy Stock Photo, p74 b Royal Mint/Getty Images, p75 Jansos/Alamy Stock Photo, p76 Chris Bull/Alamy Stock Photo, p77 l Jenny Matthews/Alamy Stock Photo, p77 r epa european pressphoto agency b.v./Alamy Stock Photo, p78 t Robert Hoetink/Shutterstock, p78 b Jeff Morgan 04/Alamy Stock Photo, p79 Art Directors & Trip/Alamy Stock Photo, p80 t North Wind Picture Archives/